FORAGING GUIDE

*How to Gather and Store Wild Plants
Throughout the Year
(2022 for Beginners)*

Clara Massy

TABLE OF CONTENT

INTRODUCTION

Historically, humans have relied on nature to survive. In fact, the first humans, who lived millions of years ago (Roberts P, 2017), were the first foragers (A., 2015) on the planet. What did they do because they were hungry and needed to survive? They went into the wilderness in search of food! They either hunted animals or gathered edible wild plants, allowing them to eat a well-balanced diet (Cordain, 2000).

It's worth noting that ancient humans gathered all of the food with their own two hands and most likely ate it right away. To meet their dietary needs, they would go in search of berries, wild greens, mushrooms, and various fruits and plants that grew in bushes.

To recognize and learn which plants were safe to eat, which were poisonous, and what types of edible wild plants could be found at specific times of the year, ancient humans had to go through a lot of trials and errors. They didn't have a book to consult or research before eating them, so imagine how difficult it was to forage for food back then!

It could be argued that modern society has lost touch with our ancestors' knowledge because we have lost the ability to forage. We are now consuming an all-time high amount of sugar (Stadterman, 2020), flours, and industrialized foods, which has resulted in a broken food system, as evidenced by looking down at everything we buy at the supermarket.

Now, I'm not here to tell you what's right or wrong about what and how we should eat or drink because it's all too subjective. However, I will state that growing food on large scale farms that are really far away from customers, so the food then has to travel for thousands of miles to reach the final destination and then the consumers can eat it, is not an ideal concept; at least, not to me.

Individuals are not only unable to see and understand how their food is grown, but they also lack an idea or a personal connection to what they eat. As a result, people have no idea how a vegetable is grown or how long it takes to reach that size. They are unaware that several edible wild plants in nature are similar – and sometimes more flavorful – to those purchased at the grocery store. And they have no idea about any of this because they have never gone foraging!

I know that going to the supermarket and buying everything is a common practice for many people. However, there is a significant movement that is now resurging in which we believe that gathering food is natural and that nature is our vast and open-air supermarket. We've grown accustomed to others imposing their fear on us because they don't know what it's like to go outside and pick some edible, nutritious, and free wild plants, but we do, and now you will, too!

Some gardeners or farmers have crops in their gardens but aren't taking full advantage of them because they either dislike going foraging or don't know how. However, if they went out and explored what other types of edible wild plants they have, their yields, nutrition, and overall health could be ten times better.

Nonetheless, there is a term used in the farming community to describe the time between winter and spring; it refers to when winter has passed and farmers are now busy organizing and planting the crops that will eventually become their food for the rest of the year. This is known as "the hungry gap."

"What now?" new gardeners always wonder. when this time of year arrives because it means that all of the fruits and vegetables they have grown are running low, particularly if they have not yet preserved any food.

Did you know, however, that successful foraging for edible wild plants is now encouraged by individual farmers? Because they understand how it can help you bridge the "hunger gap" between seasons.

In fact, there are many edible wild plants in nature, and you can find them near where you live or live. The types of wild plants you have will vary depending on where you live, but most of the time, people from all over the world have edible wild plants that they are unaware of, and they could be eating for free!

If you want to be more resilient, or if you want to supplement your already growing vegetable garden, incorporating edible wild plants into your diet will definitely help you achieve these goals, because they have nutritional value (Guarrera, 2016).

In this book, I'll show you how to find and eat different types of wild foods throughout the year. More specifically, I will walk you through the edible wild plants, which will not only keep your stomach full but may also become an important source of vitamins and nutrients throughout the year.

When you pick your own food, you know it's as fresh as it gets, but you're also reconnecting with all your ancestors who did the same thing years and years ago. You'll feel more connected to nature, and you'll be proud that you discovered something in nature. You can now secure your own food because you know it is safe, nutritious, and tasty. And, if there is ever a famine (Pinela, 2017), you will be fine if you go foraging for food!

Now, I'm not saying that harvesting edible wild plants is without risk because the reality is that it can be dangerous, especially if you go alone. We will never have the detailed and oriented knowledge that our hunter-gatherer forefathers possessed, no matter how hard we try.

As a result, we can't just go to some fields and start picking whatever plants we want to eat later. This is irresponsible because you could seriously injure yourself or even die in some cases! This is why you should always be cautious when foraging; many non-edible wild plants resemble edible wild plants, but the main difference is that they are poisonous (Cornara, 2018), so you must be cautious.

But we're all here to learn about edible wild plants. I admit that it may take years for you (or me) to learn how to correctly identify all of the different types of wild plants that can be eaten - but once you start reaping the benefits of foraging, you will never look back!

You can use this book to get answers to all of your questions. You will find incredible and relevant information on all topics related to foraging, harvesting, and storing edible wild plants. You will understand what types of plants are edible, when and where to find them, how much to eat, and all of the benefits of foraging edible wild plants.

Despite the fact that many plants are easily identified, we will go over them! If you want to start foraging with confidence, this is the book for you. We'll go over everything you need to know before foraging, harvesting, and storing edible wild plants safely and sustainably.

Foraging has many advantages, such as bringing more food to your table (thereby expanding your food options), trying new flavors (which are unlikely to be available in supermarkets), and actually saving money (of course, this will depend on your success at foraging).

Furthermore, foraging connects you to nature and may even save your life, especially if you are in a difficult situation where you must think quickly to survive. If you're prepared, you'll know what you can eat and what you should avoid.

You will also need to know what types of wild plants are not edible.

But what if you live in a big city? Edible wild plants can grow almost anywhere! Some will be visible in the cracks of a city sidewalk, but I wouldn't touch them. Edible wild plants can be found on hills, mountains, in your garden, and literally everywhere. They're just waiting for you to pick them up and eat or store them!

One of the most common misconceptions people have about foraging, harvesting, and storing their plants is that if they live in a city, they cannot do so! This is not the case!

If you live in the city, there are numerous options. Many homeowners, for example, who have fruit trees will gladly let you take some of the extra fruit that the trees produce because they cannot eat it all. You must politely request permission to harvest the fruit that has fallen to the ground before it rots. You will not only be receiving free fruit, but you will also be assisting them in maintaining a cleaner home environment! It's a win-win situation for everyone.

If you are looking for appropriate places to forage, first try it on your own land, or, if that is not possible, go to a public space (such as a park) and try to forage there. Always ask before going in if you know someone who owns the land and is okay with you foraging on it!

It's truly fascinating when people become foragers because they begin to observe nature more closely than ever before. They will soon realize what phase the moon is without having to go to a website to find out! They will also be aware that as the moon's phase changes, nature will provide a different set of plants.

As a forager, you will notice changes in your physical health; you will begin eating better and walking more frequently, which counts as exercise. You will feel like you belong because you are doing something that will undoubtedly benefit others.

Introduce yourself to a new community. Furthermore, your finances will improve because why buy garlic when you can forage, harvest, and store wild garlic?! Isn't that incredible?

When you go foraging, you do more than just walk. You see, you bend, you stretch, you dig, you search some more, you go around visualizing what you want to find, and you are always surprised by what you actually find.

When you forage your food, you always have fresh food and it costs you nothing! When you go foraging with your friends or family, you are sharing this unique experience with them as well, and this bond may extend beyond your immediate circle of people and spread into your community.

When you think about it, many of the plants we can buy at the grocery store have a mild flavor, which you will quickly realize once you start eating wild plants. In comparison to store-bought plants, these have more minerals, nutrients, antioxidants, and vitamins.

The best part is that these edible wild plants don't require any water, pesticides, or fertilizers. In fact, many of them grow on their own without our assistance. Many people regard them as "weeds," but they actually provide many benefits to our lives.

Finally, foraging, harvesting, and storing edible wild plants are enjoyable activities! You will learn about a wide variety of plants, why nature is so important, and how you can return to a simpler way of life. I understand that it can be intimidating and even frightening at first because you may not know what to consume safely.

I'm also aware that foraging isn't suitable for everyone. If you do decide to go foraging, you will quickly realize that it takes time, effort, and, most importantly, patience to train and learn about edible wild plants so that you can consume them correctly. However, if you keep going,

As you forage outdoors, you will gain experience and knowledge about which types of edible wild plants to select.

That's why I wrote this book for you; I've had you on my mind for a long time! My goal is to teach you how to go outside and start noticing and observing nature so that you, too, can start gathering edible wild plants right away.

So, if you want to learn more about foraging, harvesting, and storing edible wild plants throughout the year, guess what? You shouldn't look any further because this comprehensive guide will teach you everything you need to know about edible wild plants (as well as non-edible wild plants!)

Best wishes, I sincerely hope you have a good time!

CHAPTER: 1

Beginners' Guide to Food Foraging

If you want to start foraging for edible wild plants, you should first understand some of the basics.

When considering foraging, a person may consider mushrooms, fruits, vegetables, herbs, or any other medicinal plant found in nature. Foraging for food is not as difficult as some people believe; in fact, with this guide, you will be able to identify various types of edible wild plants.

This chapter will teach you everything you need to know about food foraging for beginners!

The Advantages of Foraging Your Own Food

There are numerous advantages to foraging your own food. The following are some of the most important, as they are shared by the majority of foragers:

You're Experimenting with New Flavors

When eating edible wild plants, you will quickly notice how different they taste from what we are used to eating. However, you will notice that these new flavors will never be available at your local grocery store.

Foraging is an opportunity (and one you give yourself) to try unusual and tasty plants that provide new flavors (Cornara, 2018). And you can experiment with them to make a variety of dishes; so, if you're planning a dinner party soon, don't forget to go foraging before everyone arrives!

You are eating free food.

If you foraged for your food, you almost certainly spent nothing to obtain it! Foraging for food is an excellent idea if you are on a tight budget or simply want to save some money each month.

What's ironic is that if you do end up finding your foraged plants in the supermarket, they'll most likely be expensive. Consider mushrooms, for example! (I know they aren't plants, but I want you to understand this point.) When foraging for mushrooms, you can find them in many parts of the world.

If you buy the same mushrooms at your local store, you'll notice how much more expensive they are! Pine nuts are another example of something you can easily find for free when foraging, but they are expensive when sold in supermarkets.

You're Eating Well

Edible wild plants are an excellent source of nutrition. To give you an example, wild dandelion plants contain more phytonutrients than store-bought spinach; however, people dislike weeds so much that they try to remove them from their gardens whenever possible!

Furthermore, when you are out in nature foraging for food, your body benefits as well. You will not only be walking around but you will also be exposed to the sun, which is a good source of vitamin D.

Finally, you will begin to pay attention to what you put into your body, how you feed yourself, what your body accepts or rejects, and what makes you feel good — being healthy begins when you love yourself so much that your diet is balanced!

You are working out.

Foraging for food can be considered a sport, albeit not a high-intensity one, but going outside will still benefit you.

When you start looking for edible wild plants, you probably walk a lot, are constantly moving, and sometimes even hike to high places to harvest your food.

But you're also reaching for some fruits, bending to identify and gather some greens, and going from one place to another picking up things!

Foraging for food is, in my opinion, a better form of exercise than going to the gym! And if you combine hunting with growing your own vegetables, that's it! You're working out every muscle in your body, including your tongue!

You are making a connection with nature.

If you pick your own food, you will know where that fruit (or other produce) came from; this will make you feel more connected to nature because you are consuming something you saw and knew was there where you harvested it.

When you become an experienced forager, you will understand when it is best to forage for edible plants. You know how their flavor changes with the season (or even the moon phase), and how much some of those plants will grow (or be stunted) if they don't get enough sun or water.

Even though you are observing, you are not simply observing nature because you are acting alongside it and consuming what it provides. This connection to nature is something that almost all of us have lost because it is definitely lost in the modern world where everything needs to be done right now, and as a result, we have an agriculture system in which crops are constantly being introduced to fertilizers to grow faster than ever before.

You are putting sustainability into action.

When foraging, you select plants that are locally grown, organic, and free. You are not spending your money on purchasing fruits and vegetables from other parts of the world.

Because you are not using harmful pesticides or other types of hazardous agricultural chemicals, the plants are "better," and you are not harming nature by foraging these plants.

In fact, the inverse occurs. Because you don't have to water the plants; the rain does. You are not reliant on fossil fuels to forage those plants, and your carbon footprint is significantly reduced.

Furthermore, because you are utilizing local resources, you may be regarded as a garden hero (at least to me!). You're foraging plants to eat, and some of them are commonly regarded as weeds, so people try to avoid them at all costs.

As you can see, foraging for food is necessary, enjoyable, and provides numerous benefits. And the most important paradigm you will ever challenge once you begin foraging for food is that food is everywhere. Contrary to popular belief, it is not limited to supermarkets or vegetable gardens! If you spend enough time and effort observing nature, you will notice food everywhere.

The Dangers of Foraging for Edible Wild Plants

Foraging for food, on the other hand, comes with a big red warning sign. If you are unsure about the plant, avoid eating it. It is always best to correctly identify the plant before consuming it; otherwise, serious consequences may result.

Other risks of foraging edible wild plants include:

Too much information can be perplexing.

To become a forager, you must first learn to identify edible wild plants, but you must also learn to identify non-edible plants. You may feel as though there is a lot of information floating around, which may confuse you because you don't know where to begin.

Fortunately, this guide is now available! We will go over all of the pertinent and necessary information that will assist you in successfully foraging for food.

You Must Deal With and Overcome Unfamiliarity

Strangely, unfamiliar foods can bring back a lot of old memories. Consider this: as toddlers, we were probably too excited every time we saw a new food or were too afraid to even touch it!

When you first start foraging, you will come across many unfamiliar foods, and if you try them without properly cooking or preparing them, you will most likely put them back and never eat them again!

It's almost as important to know how to eat the plants you find in the wilderness as it is to know which plants are safe for human consumption. In fact, many edible wild plants are bitter, don't taste good when eaten raw, and some are even indigestible if not cooked properly.

If you are a novice forager, make sure you understand how to use the plants you are harvesting; otherwise, all of the product you just harvested will go to waste in a matter of days because you will be turned off by their taste or texture.

You Might Select a "Bad" Plant

When a person first begins foraging, the first question he or she asks is, "Am I picking the right edible wild plant?" Because, even if you have this guide with you, you will occasionally wonder whether that is the same plant or whether it is edible or not.

If you're not careful, you might end up eating something poisonous because some wild plants are poisonous! Nobody is immune to this, as it can happen to even the most experienced forager.

Furthermore, even if you are certain that the plant you just harvested is completely safe and non-toxic, they can still be filled, pesticide residues, and even animal waste This is why it is critical to thoroughly rinse them before consumption (even if you are in your garden or land).

You may be endangering the environment where you harvest.

As foragers, we will do everything we can to preserve nature. However, sometimes we are unaware of situations that are taking place beneath the plants we are attempting to harvest.

For example, if we are new to foraging, we may not be aware of how much of the plant we can take without causing harm. Plants may perish as a result of our harvesting intrusion. Other times, we take so much of one plant that it becomes weakened, and another more robust and invasive species emerges. Finally, we may be walking on delicate soil, crushing plants without realizing it, or unknowingly disrupting habitats.

Some areas are extremely sensitive, and we risk causing severe damage if we go in and harvest their plants. It is always necessary to keep this possibility in mind because we are not foraging in order to destroy habitats!

Some areas make foraging illegal.

I know it sounds insane! How is foraging illegal? How can you be arrested if you're just gathering food? However, in some parts of the world, foraging appears to be incompatible with modern life.

On the other hand, if you try to harvest on another person's property without permission, you will get in trouble because it is their private property.

On the other hand, it's not like you can just go somewhere public and start foraging again; in fact, many parks forbid you from taking any plants! There are also restrictions on how much of a specific plant you can take in some places.

As you can see, it's best if you know what the laws are where you live before you start foraging; this way, you'll avoid any awkward situations where you end up inside a police car!

Foods That Can Be Foraged

If you thought plants were the only thing you could forage, you'd be wrong! Fortunately for all of us, this is not the case! In fact, there are other foods you could easily forage for, such as mushrooms, shellfish (oysters or any other related edible shellfish), and various types of nuts.

Furthermore, did you know that it's legal in some areas to forage for food - specifically meat - if you come across a roadkill animal? However, you must ensure that the carcass is fresh. Otherwise, you risk becoming very ill.

However, if you hit an animal (such as a deer) or saw another car hit it while the carcass was still fresh, you could go forage for that meat. Make sure you understand the local laws; it is sometimes illegal to have a dead animal without a special permit. If you do decide to cook it, make sure you thoroughly cook it to kill any bacteria that may be present.

On the other hand, you should try to become acquainted with the ecosystem in which you live. Make sure you understand the different types of weeds, trees, herbs, fruits, vegetables, and flowers around you; there are many edible flowers, fungi, aquatic plants, weeds, trees, and shrubs!

If you're going foraging for the first time, try to go with someone who already knows how to do it; this way, you'll have an extra set of hands, eyes, and brains to help you! Chickweed, plantain, henbit, dandelions, wild garlic, redbud, wood sorrel, wild onions, oyster mushrooms, and many more are examples of foraged plants.

Finally, you could forage for insects and worms. They will apparently add a lot of protein to your diet! This is why they are such a valuable protein source in many parts of the world - just make sure you cook them properly!

Your Diet and Foraging

Going foraging is a significant step toward becoming more self-sufficient in terms of your dietary needs and overall health. If you grow your own food, you already know that what you eat comes directly from your garden to your table, and nothing will ever beat that feeling of satisfaction. If, on the other hand, you are not growing your own food but are considering foraging, you should do so as well - it will give you a new perspective on life!

When you begin foraging, you become aware of the importance of fresh produce, but you also become aware of the incorrect use of pesticides that farmers all over the world make when growing food. You may also be aware of the number of chemicals contained in the product you recently purchased. All of these are compelling reasons to adopt a more self-sufficient lifestyle, which you will achieve once you begin foraging for food.

Living in this manner will, in turn, make you more in tune with nature, your surroundings, and, ultimately, yourself. You will begin to appreciate every bite of food you consume, and you will be amazed at what nature is capable of.

Edible wild plants are high in nutritional value.

Most importantly, wild plants contain a high concentration of vitamins and minerals that are beneficial to human consumption and health. Indeed, some of these plants contain more nutrients than other fruits and vegetables that we are accustomed to eating!

When you think about it, this is quite ironic. We frequently pay exorbitant prices for food imported from other countries, but most of us are unaware of how close to home we can find it.

How to Begin Foraging for Wild Plants

If you want to discover new and more sustainable ways of living, you should definitely go foraging. You will not only regain food sovereignty, but you will also learn new skills and information as you are in constant contact with nature, learning about the full range of edible wild plants that exist in your area. So, how do you get started foraging for food?

Because you're reading this book, you've already gotten a head start on your foraging adventure! I recommend that you go to your backyard (if you have one) and look for the plants you are already familiar with. Don't worry if you don't have a garden! You could visit a friend's house or go to the park.

Try to observe nature as closely as possible and identify as many wild plants as you can. You'll be surprised at how much (or how little) you actually know! However, the purpose of this exercise is not to make you feel bad about your lack of knowledge; remember, this is a long journey, and we are all constantly learning!

After that, broaden your foraging horizons! Visit a different park, a family member's garden, or a botanical garden, watch videos online, look for images of the plants you were able to identify at the start, and, most importantly, immerse yourself in knowledge and information!

Prepare yourself! I know you can pull it off!

What Equipment Do You Require?

Going foraging for food is a simple yet enjoyable activity that requires no special equipment. It would be ideal if you had a notepad, a pen, a field guide, a small knife for weeds, a large knife for roots, a small pruner for herbs, kitchen scissors, and a magnifying glass.

A digging fork, a zip-lock bag (or several), a basket or cloth bag, and a small shovel are all required.

Because I am a very visual person, I will always recommend a camera! When I first began foraging, I would photograph the plant and then compare it to the ones in my field guide. I'd also ask my friends, who were more experienced than me at the time when it came to foraging for food.

If we were successful in obtaining the correct information about the foraged plant, I would write it down on my notepad and print the photograph to place next to the description. This has always been a great exercise because it has allowed me to learn (and, more importantly, remember!) everything about the plants I've come across.

Where to Look for Wild Edible Plants

You could go wild edible plant foraging anywhere in the world! If you live in the city and plan to go foraging, keep the following tips in mind:

Stay away from contaminated areas.

You must consider the areas where you will go foraging and whether or not they have contaminants that could be harmful to your health. If you live in a polluted area with a lot of pollution, I recommend you avoid foraging there.

When you first start foraging, make sure you go to areas far away from human activity, so going to the countryside is a great idea!

Avoid crowded public parks.

I know I've already told you to go to a park if you don't have a garden, and you can still go if you're just starting out with foraging and can't identify your first couple of plants.

However, if you feel ready and want to harvest some edible wild plants, you should avoid busy public parks because they are likely to be contaminated (even if there isn't trash all over the place!).

This pollution is frequently invisible to the naked eye, but the plants you want to eat are likely contaminated with heavy toxins that can harm your immune system. So, if you're serious about eating your foraged food, avoid congested public parks!

Avoid Dog Zones

You should also avoid areas where dogs are known to 'do their business.' In fact, you should avoid any other areas where any type of animal urinates. This could seriously infect nearby plants, and thus seriously infect you with a disease or something similar.

When Should You Go Foraging for Edible Wild Plants?

Imagine going foraging and thinking you want to eat a specific type of plant, only to discover that the time for that plant to sprout has passed!

It is critical to correctly identify plants so that you will know when they are growing and producing fruits for you to forage and consume.

It's also important to know when plants bloom, because if you're unsure about one or two plants but know they bloom in May and it's now July, you'll know you're looking at two different species that look alike.

Knowing about plants will also provide you with another advantage: you will be aware of the various times plants take to flower or produce fruit, as well as when to harvest.

If the plant you are looking for is not performing as it should (in your opinion), you should always seek the advice of an expert.

Before eating the plant Otherwise, you could endanger yourself.

Furthermore, harvest edible wild plants whenever you suspect the plant is "oily." This indicates that they are actively releasing their aroma, and their flavor will be much stronger as a result. Of course, this is a matter of personal preference! If you want to take advantage of the plant's nutritional content, however, it is best to harvest it before it flowers, as it will be full of nutrients, vitamins, and minerals.

Here are some general guidelines to follow:

It is preferable to harvest the plants before they flower; otherwise, they will lack nutrients.

It's best to harvest when you see the plant has enough foliage; this way, you'll help her continue to grow.

You should harvest early in the morning or as the sun sets. Harvesting should not be done in the afternoon, when the heat of the day is at its peak!

Improving Your Foraging Capabilities

Assume you've recently begun "foraging." It was your first time, and you did exactly what I said: you only identified plants you already knew. You realized that nature is providing you with superfoods right in your own backyard! You also realized how much you want to keep foraging for your own food.

The next step will be to improve your foraging abilities so that you don't make as many mistakes while out and about.

I'd like to remind you that you're honing and learning these important foraging skills. Historically, all of our ancestors, regardless of nationality, were constantly consuming wild foods to survive. They were the first to recognize the medicinal properties of plants.

They were able to save lives simply by consuming and using (or applying topically) plants!

Our forefathers all lived through periods of war, illness, and, in some cases, famine. And, despite having lost touch with nature, we are now returning to our roots, practicing regenerative farming because we care about our soils, and actively welcoming nature's changes into our lives.

Improving our foraging skills also entails being aware of the thousands or millions of wild plants that are excellent to consume or apply if we want to support our immune system and improve our health.

You should be aware that the more foraging you do, the more confident you will become. Finding edible wild plants is not difficult; you just need to be in the right frame of mind when exploring.

What to Wear When Wild Plant Foraging

I was wearing a dress and flip-flops the first time I went foraging for food! And, no, I don't recommend dressing similarly to this when you go foraging! It was the beginning of summer, and I had no idea I'd be spending the day in the wilderness hunting for food.

Don't get me wrong: I had a great time, and this experience opened my eyes and made me realize how much I didn't know about plants, as well as made me happy about how much I could now learn about those plants!

I went with a couple of experts who had been there a few days before our visit. You must surround yourself with other foragers, especially at the start, when everything appears to be too new and confusion reigns supreme!

Wear comfortable clothing if you intend to go foraging for food. Dress appropriately for the season; however, even in the middle of summer, I would recommend

If you don't wear long sleeves and pants, insects will devour you in no time!

You should also wear a hat and comfortable shoes. You'll probably be walking and moving around a lot, so you'll need to be able to move freely; otherwise, you'll have a difficult time out in nature.

Foraging in Groups vs. Solitary

If this is your first time foraging for food, you should definitely go with someone else or even a group of people. I would also recommend that you find someone who is knowledgeable about plant identification and willing to teach you.

If you go alone, the whole thing can seem overwhelming at first, and you're likely to give up, especially if you come across a plant that looks similar. As a result, always go with someone who is knowledgeable about food identification.

Even if you feel confident enough to go alone, you should always choose to go with someone else. Although foraging for plants is not as dangerous as foraging for wild mushrooms, you should still exercise caution whenever you try a new plant.

It would be preferable if you also respected any future visitors who may come to the location where you are foraging (unless you are foraging in your garden). Other foragers will undoubtedly go there, so always leave with all your litter and try to be as respectful as possible, both to nature and to other foragers.

CHAPTER 2

Basic Rules of Foraging Wild Plants

As a new forager, you may have a lot of questions about what to eat, how to harvest the plants, and the basic rules of foraging food!

To be completely honest, even if you are a seasoned forager, there will always be something new to learn because nature is vast. Every day, we learn about new plants.

These are not rules that everyone must follow; however, if we all followed them, it would mean that we are all taking care of this planet and its sometimes-limited resources!

These are unspoken rules, but that doesn't make them any less important to follow and teach to other foragers whenever possible. Here are some ground rules for when we go foraging:

Setting out on your first foraging expedition

Foraging can appear difficult at first, especially if you are in the middle of a forest looking for wild edibles. It is a challenge you must be willing to accept because you will be surrounded by an abundance of edible roots, berries, nuts, and plants. So, what are your options? Where should you begin?

You should always begin by exploring and seeing if you recognize any of the plants you see. Take your time, but inspect everything thoroughly (or at least, as much as possible).

If you're going with someone who is more experienced, ask them! Do they agree that this plant is similar to the one you described? Or do they believe it's a completely different one? In any case, always pay attention to what they say and compare it to yours and any other relevant guides you may have.

Endangered Species must be protected.

One of the first times I went foraging, I came across a lovely fruit tree. It was small, but it had the biggest oranges I'd ever seen in my life, or so I thought. I was about to take a "orange" when my friend stopped me and asked what that fruit was. "Is it an orange?" I asked, and she replied, "No, it's not an orange." In this small community, it is one of the endangered species. We can't take it anymore."

I felt terrible because I was about to bring those oranges with me, even though I had no idea what this particular fruit meant in the context we were in.

That day, I learned an important lesson: always respect endangered species! Furthermore, foraging for endangered species is illegal in many parts of the world, and you could even go to jail for it!

Discover the Plants

However, in order to respect endangered species, you must first understand what they are.

Before eating a plant, try to identify it. You should also be aware that plants in real life may appear slightly different from plants in a book. This principle also applies to the same plants found in different locations and climates; they may appear similar to you, but they differ.

Check with a local expert, who should be someone from the area who is also knowledgeable about foraging. So, if you don't know something, always ask someone else!

Identification of edible wild plants may improve your experience. On the contrary, if the identification process was flawed, it could have serious consequences!

Finally, as you are probably aware, many fruits and vegetables grow during a specific season, as do these edible wild plants!

Dandelions, for example, will not be available in the fall. If you do, you might not see as many of them, or they might taste different!

This is why it's important to know what kinds of edible wild plants grow during the season you're in. This way, you'll be aware of which plants you'll be consuming, and your foraging experience will be more likely to be successful.

Discover the Zones

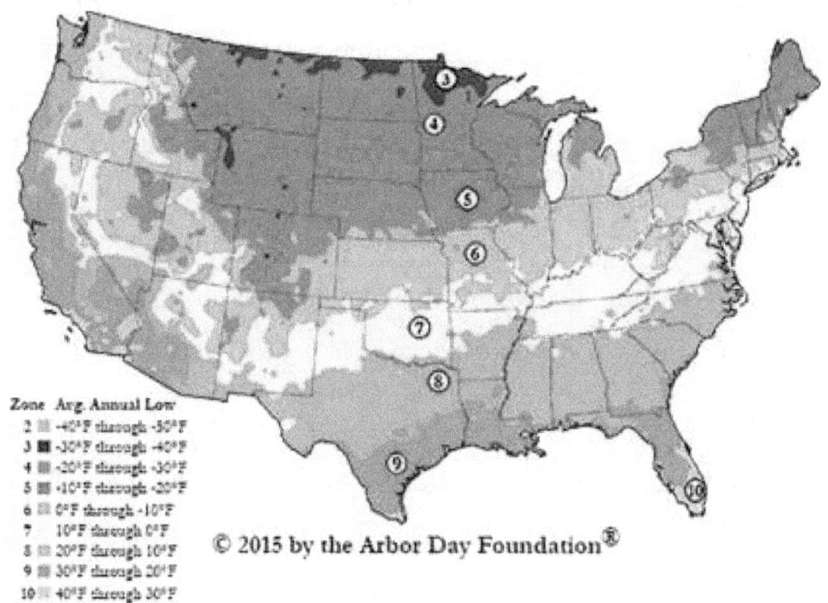

The USDA hardiness zone is a concept used in the United States of America. This colorful zone map will be one of the most useful tools you will ever come across, as it will explain which planting or growing zone you are in. As a new forager, this will help you understand the climate in your area. Then you'll need to do some research to figure out which plants are nearby and which can survive.

This map depicts the country's hardiness zones and is based on the average annual extreme minimum temperature recorded in specific areas over the last 30 years.

Obviously, this is only a "rough" guide, as new microclimates may emerge that are simply too difficult to depict on a map. On the other hand, it is possible for one location to have two different zones because it is bordered by another USDA hardiness zone.

This is an excellent tool to have because it will be useful whenever you need to see the "bigger picture." However, this should never be used to replace knowledge gained from simply observing your garden or any other open-spaced area nearby, especially if you are foraging.

Knowing which type of zone you are in is critical for foraging success. Consider going foraging and believing that you are in x zone. You get excited because you saw a plant and thought you recognized it right away, so you give it a try and eat it. But then, as you do more research, you realize you're in zone z, and that plant you just ate doesn't grow there! You either ate another plant or an anomaly occurred in that location, causing the plant to appear. You must exercise caution in either case!

Edible Wild Plant Foraging and Sustainability

To me, the beauty of foraging is that you are aware of the plants in front of you, you know what you are doing, and how nature works, and you can feed yourself and your loved ones as a result.

You will satisfy your hunger while also meeting your inner call because you are doing something that few people are willing to do nowadays.

Here are some of the fundamental sustainable principles associated with food foraging:

Always depart with something.

If you go foraging, try to leave something behind. To put it another way, don't take more than you need. By doing so, you will not only leave something for future foragers, but you will also leave something for yourself.

You will not only be looking after yourself, but you will also be ensuring that plants do not die immediately after you take them.

When you leave some plants behind, you should protect the environment from which the plants were taken. They can also propagate themselves in this manner, resulting in more of the same plant.

If you begin foraging ethically and sustainably, you and other foragers will be able to use the same location for a longer period of time.

Do Not Remove the Roots

If at all possible, try to leave the root systems of the plants alone; this way, the plants will continue to grow even if you have already taken some of the leaves or upper parts of the plant.

You are also respecting the plant if you leave the roots, even if it provides plenty of other plants. Instead of taking one whole plant, try taking two or three leaves from different plants.

Also, proceed with caution; you can use a small knife instead of doing everything by hand. If you are not cautious and take or slice into the plant's roots, you may kill it.

Keep an eye out for overharvesting.

Overharvesting is a serious problem in foraging communities. Many foragers believe that if a plant has grown in a specific location, they can take it all and it will regrow, because that's how nature works, right?

But it isn't. When a forager takes all of a plant, it may never grow again. Some say it's because foragers have completely disrespected the plants, while others blame the soil; in any case, we shouldn't be overharvesting it all; rather, we should only take what we truly need.

Also, if you harvest from a specific patch, let it grow before harvesting from it again. These plants will need to recover before their numbers are reduced again.

Many people used to go foraging for plants all over the world, and now those same plants are nearly extinct! We should be plant protectors, not planet destroyers!

All Ecosystems Must Be Respected

Perhaps you consider some plants to be weeds because they are invasive and spread uncontrollably. Have you ever considered whether they are there for a reason? People, for example, consider clovers to be weeds, and many will go to great lengths to destroy them if they see any.

But did you know that clovers are actually beneficial to the soil? They return some nitrogen to the earth, which is always beneficial! Furthermore, they are an excellent source of nutrients for humans to consume. So, the next time you consider pulling some "insignificant weeds," consider clovers and their significance!

Knowing your local ecosystems is important because you will know which plants are native, which are invasive, and which will either deplete or provide nutrients to the ground.

The more you understand a plant's ecosystem, the better you'll be able to decide whether or not to forage for it. It is sometimes best to leave them alone because they are there for a reason!

Protected Areas Should Be Maintained

Do not go foraging for food in a national park or nature reserve! These areas are all protected, especially if there are many wild animals present. Remember that this is their space, not ours, and that they are the ones who are safe, not us.

It is sometimes illegal to forage from these areas as well; therefore, if you go to protected land, make sure you are aware of all foraging laws.

You Should Plant Back If Possible

I understand that edible wild plants are, well, wild for a reason! However, if possible, you can spread the seeds of native species found where you go foraging throughout the soil and into the air.

Even though you are interfering, you are also giving something back because nature will do its job and, hopefully, those seeds will begin to grow as well.

Don't Choose the Small Ones

Or the ones that aren't growing well. It may seem obvious, but I have seen it many times before: some foragers will take most, if not all, of the plants that are left! That is why I advise you to only harvest plants that are abundantly growing.

Be Aware of Your Surrounding Environment

When foraging, try to protect any nearby species that may be found near the plants you are harvesting. You should also avoid disturbing the nests or even the homes of any animals that may be living in that area; otherwise, you could seriously harm their ecosystem.

Some animals are extremely sensitive, as in they have been through a lot and may be scared if they see you foraging near where they live. Make sure you respect them, as well as the plants they may consume.

Invite others to join you foraging.

Foraging is a wonderful pastime for many of us. It combines everything we enjoy: we get to exercise, practice our memory and observation skills, connect with nature, and end up eating or consuming extremely healthy and nutritious food for free.

If you like foraging, you should invite others to join you! You will be passing knowledge from one to another by teaching others what you already know. You will also be sharing your appreciation for nature with others, and you may even have a greater impact.

When you go foraging, form a bond with that person. Foraging edible wild plants sustainably is a wonderful gift you can give to anyone you care about! It is unquestionably a difficult skill that we should all learn at a young age!

CHAPTER: 3

Everything You Should Know About Edible Wild Plants In Spring

Oh, springtime! Who doesn't enjoy the scent of newly blooming flowers? The sun is gradually emerging, the trees are waking up, and the animals are coming out to play!

Everything grows in the spring! Personally, I believe it is the most changing season because it gradually transitions from winter to spring and everything begins to thaw until the warm sun returns!

Spring is an excellent time to begin foraging edible wild plants because winter has passed and it is neither too cold nor too hot. It is also an excellent time for plants to begin sprouting all over.

This chapter will teach you everything you need to know about Edible Spring Wild Plants. You'll learn how to eat your greens, which ones to harvest in the early spring, and which ones to cook before eating:

What You Should Know About Spring Foraging

When Spring arrives, all plants will begin to bloom. Some greens will sprout, and you may find nutrient-dense plants waiting for you right at your feet.

Some people prefer to wait a little longer before beginning to forage, but I believe that the beginning of Spring brings a plethora of different and delicious plants for us to enjoy, such as garlic mustard.

Many people will find these plants too bitter at the end of the season, and they are; this is why you will either have to get used to the taste or consume most plants at the start of the season.

Going foraging in the spring is fantastic because you will be able to walk in nice weather, see how everything is growing, and make wonderful memories.

Types of Edible Wild Plants Available This Season

Even though the season for edible wild plants appears to be very short (because they were dormant during winter and now summer is approaching), you will still be able to find a wide variety of edible plants.

Let's take a look at what you might be able to forage during this time of year.

Wild Onions

Easily one of my favorite edible wild plants! And I believe that every beginner in the foraging world enjoys them because they are relatively easy to identify. Wild onions are one of the first plants to sprout in the spring, and if you live in the eastern United States, you will almost certainly see them around this time. They are also extremely medicinal (Aleksandar, 2019).

Important note: Wild onions can be eaten raw! Simply sprinkle them over any dish you're cooking, and you're done! Your food will taste even better as a result.

How to Collect it. When harvesting, only pick the tops and leave the roots in the ground; this way, you'll have a steady supply of wild onions for a long time. You should harvest them in the early spring.

How to Keep It. Allow them to dry naturally before storing them in a paper bag or jars with tight lids in a cool, dry, dark place. You should label the container with the plant's name and the date you collected it. Mold is very likely to grow in plastic bags.

Keep in mind that plants retain their properties for the first year, so marking the container with the date is essential. Alternatively, you can combine it with oil and place it in ice cube trays before freezing them. When you want to use it, simply take it out and let it cook alongside the rest of the food.

Garlic Mustard

Alliaria petiolate is the scientific name for this plant. Although this plant is native to Europe, it has spread all over the world and is now considered an invasive species in the United States...which is great news for us foragers! You will not only be able to go foraging for this plant, but if it is that invasive, you will be able to take a large number of them and control its spread!

How to Collect it. You simply need to carefully remove it from the soil. You should harvest them throughout the spring, depending on the weather.

Depending on your zone, you may be able to harvest it during the summer as well.

How to Keep It. Allow them to dry naturally before storing them in a paper bag or jars with tight lids in a cool, dry, dark place. You should label the container with the plant's name and the date you collected it. Mold is very likely to grow in plastic bags.

Keep in mind that plants retain their properties for the first year, so marking the container with the date is essential. Alternatively, you can combine it with oil and place it in ice cube trays before freezing them. When you want to use it, simply take it out and let it cook alongside the rest of the food.

Wild Garlic

Allium ursinum is its scientific name. Another one of my favorite plants! Wild garlic has a strong flavor, but it is delicious! If you were able to forage some, thoroughly wash the plant and chop the leaves. Your entire house will now stink of wild garlic!

You can chop them and use them in salads; in fact, their leaves can be used in a variety of dishes. It is also safe to eat its flowers and bulbs; it has been reported that this type of wild garlic aids in healing.

Important note: Wild garlic juice can also be used as a household disinfectant. How awesome is that? It will even assist you in keeping pests out of your garden.

How to Collect it

You can eat the entire plant if you want to, which means you can harvest the entire plant in one go if necessary. You simply need to carefully remove it from the soil. They should be harvested throughout the spring.

How to Keep It. Allow them to dry naturally before storing them in a paper bag or jars with tight lids in a cool, dry, dark place. You should label the container with the plant's name and the date you collected it. Mold is very likely to grow in plastic bags.

Keep in mind that plants retain their properties for the first year, so marking the container with the date is essential. Alternatively, you can combine it with oil and place it in ice cube trays before freezing them. When you want to use it, simply take it out and let it cook alongside the rest of the food.

Thimbleberry Shoots

Rubus parviflorus is the scientific name for this plant. The Pacific Northwest of the United States is home to this plant. It is similar to raspberry in that it contains wild red berries. The fruits, on the other hand, will take a long time to mature, and you may be able to eat them at the end of fall.

How to Collect it. At the start of spring, you could eat the leaves or even the young shoots.

How to Keep It. Pull the leaves in your fridge just like you would other types of green leaves. If not, allow them to dry naturally before storing them in a paper bag or jars with tight lids in a cool, dry, dark place. You should label the container with the plant's name and the date you collected it. Mold is very likely to grow in plastic bags.

Keep in mind that plants retain their properties for the first year, so marking the container with the date is essential. Alternatively, you can combine it with oil and place it in ice cube trays before freezing them. When you want to use it, simply take it out and let it cook alongside the rest of the food.

Flowers of Dandelion

Taraxacum is its scientific name. Dandelions, despite their appearance, are extremely tough plants! They will even begin to appear before the snow (or cold weather) has completely melted.

Another distinguishing feature is that they only appear for a short period of time; thus, they appear, and ten minutes later, they are all gone!

Many farmers regard dandelions as an invasive species; however, they contribute numerous beneficial minerals to the soil. If you forage for dandelions in the early spring, you can eat them raw. If not, they will become bitter over time.

If you wanted to, you could eat the entire plant. They do, however, have a strong, bitter taste, so consume them while they are still young (or cook them!).

Finally, some people have experimented with dandelions and made wine! It appears to be very good as well! So, if you have the chance and see some dandelions nearby, pick them and make some wine!

Important note: This plant is also known as a diuretic plant; it contains many vitamins such as A, C, E, and K; and you can drink the dried leaves as a tea. They are especially beneficial if you have diabetes (Wirngo, 2016).

How to Collect it.

Depending on what you want to do with the flowers, you only need to cut the flowers or the entire plant. If you want to make a salad, vinegar, or tea, you should harvest the leaf. If you want to make a stronger-flavored vinegar, tincture, or decoction, on the other hand, you should harvest the roots. If you plan to eat them raw, harvest them in the early spring; otherwise, harvest them throughout the season.

How to Keep It.

The roots of dandelions are edible. I usually dry and grind them before adding them to my milk, and it truly tastes like coffee! Place it in a hermetic container where no air can pass through before storing it in your cupboard!

Dollar Weed

Hydrocotyle spp. is another name for it. This plant is a typical example of a plant that goes to waste because many people are unaware that it is edible. In fact, whenever it appears in a garden, people immediately remove it because if not, the entire garden will be overrun with dollar weeds!

But hold on a second! What if you ate the dollar weed instead of throwing it away to rot? Because we will be eating nutritious food, this will be extremely beneficial to both our health and the environment!

This plant has a flavor similar to carrots and celery. You could easily cook with it, but only use the leaves; otherwise, the stems and roots will take a long time to soften.

How to Collect it.

You must be cautious when harvesting it because it is easily broken. They should be harvested throughout the spring.

How to Keep It.

It should be stored similarly to carrots or celery. Some people will store them in the refrigerator, while others will store them in a cupboard or another similar location.

King Henry the Third

Blitum bonus-henricus is the scientific name for this plant. This edible wild plant has so many benefits that it's no surprise it's nicknamed "poor man's asparagus." Many people consider it a weed, but the entire plant is truly magnificent because it has so many health benefits.

Important note: You can cut the stems (or shoots) off and cook them like asparagus. Alternatively, cut the leaves and use them in salads. Furthermore, you can harvest the seeds, soak them overnight, and then thoroughly rinse them to remove all saponins: you could eat them like quinoa! They contain a significant amount of protein.

How to Collect it.

You could collect the seeds, stems, or leaves. You can eat the entire plant if you want, and they are best harvested in the spring.

How to Keep It.

It is entirely up to you. You could either put it in the fridge or put it in the cupboard.

Elderflower

They can be found on the tree known scientifically as Sambucus nigra. These tiny flowers have a strong fragrance and can be used to make a tasty herbal tea. If you have hay fever or sinusitis, you should drink this tea (Mikulic-Petkovsek, 2015). They also make you feel relaxed, so avoid them if you plan on driving.

Important note: You can eat them raw, powdered, or dried. You can make jams and jellies, tea, and even ice cream!

How to Collect it.

You should harvest them in the early spring.

How to Keep It.

Allow them to dry naturally before storing them in a paper bag or jars with tight lids in a cool, dry, dark place. You should label the container with the plant's name and the date you collected it. Mold is very likely to grow in plastic bags.

Keep in mind that plants retain their properties for the first year, so marking the container with the date is essential.

Nettles (Stinging Nettles)

Urtica dioica is the scientific name for this plant. Another simple plant to identify in the spring. Spring nettles will also appear before the winter is over. You must wear gloves if you intend to harvest them! Otherwise, the plant will harm your hands!

Stinging nettles are known to be high in nutrients. They are similar to spinach in appearance and contain high levels of calcium, iron, magnesium, and manganese. As a superfood, you should consume a portion of this plant at least once a week (Esposito, 2019).

This plant will aid in the removal of heavy toxins from your body, the clearing of your urine, and the relief of arthritic and joint pain.

Important note: Always pick the smaller or younger leaves because they are the freshest.

Be aware: Some people may claim that they cannot consume stinging nettles because they will get a sore throat (especially those who suffer from emphysema).

Other plants, such as marshmallow plants, can be added to counteract this effect. String nettles may also affect a person's blood sugar levels, so if you have diabetes, keep this in mind.

How to Collect it

If you're worried about the stings, don't be. You can easily soak them in water, and the stings will quickly disappear. They should be harvested throughout the spring.

How to Keep It.

Allow them to dry naturally before storing them in a paper bag or jars with tight lids in a cool, dry, dark place. You should label the container with the plant's name and the date you collected it. Mold is very likely to grow in plastic bags.

Keep in mind that plants retain their properties for the first year, so marking the container with the date is essential.

Chickweed

Stellaria media is another name for Stellaria media. Many people disregard them because they are sometimes too small. Did you know, however, that the leaves are edible? You can use them in any salad at any time of year! Also, if you have insect bites, you can add chickweed to any lotion or simply rub it on the bite. Its flowers are also edible, especially at the start of spring.

Important note: If you're looking to make pesto, look no further! You don't even need basil to make a flavorful pesto now that chickweed is available!

Be aware that chickweed contains many oxalates that may interfere with your mineral intake; in other words, consuming chickweed on a regular basis may increase the formation of kidney stones.

How to Collect it.

They should be harvested throughout the spring. You only need to take what you intend to consume or eat, so grab some scissors and cut back a few inches; your food will now taste better!

How to Keep It.

Allow them to dry naturally before storing them in a paper bag or jars with tight lids in a cool, dry, dark place. You should label the container with the plant's name and the date you collected it. Mold is very likely to grow in plastic bags.

Keep in mind that plants retain their properties for the first year, so marking the container with the date is essential. Alternatively, you can combine it with oil and place it in ice cube trays before freezing them. When you want to use it, simply take it out and let it cook alongside the rest of the food.

Burdock

It is also known as Arctium. This enormous plant grows wild in many parts of the world. You could easily spot a couple of these if you go hiking in the countryside! If you eat the seeds, you are purifying your blood; burdocks also have diuretic properties, can help you get rid of heavy metal poisoning, and can help with snake bites.

Important note: Burdock roots are similar to carrot roots and can be used as a root vegetable.

How to Collect it.

Because they are a root plant, you must carefully remove them from the soil. They should be harvested throughout the spring.

How to Keep It.

If you want to keep them, don't put them in the fridge because they're used to being outside.

Hawthorn

Because hawthorn berries contain a high percentage of cyanide, they should only be consumed if you know how to safely remove the seeds (which could be detrimental to our health). Other fruits, such as apples and apricots, contain cyanide as well, and the seeds should be avoided at all costs. However, it is a little more difficult to ignore the seeds in hawthorn berries because they cover almost the entire fruit!

Important note: Thoroughly rinse the hawthorn plants.

How to Collect it.

The leaves of the Hawthorn are edible, but only when spring has arrived. Otherwise, you won't like them as much because they have a woody flavor.

How to Keep It.

Allow them to dry naturally before storing them in a paper bag or jars with tight lids in a cool, dry, dark place. You should label the container with the plant's name and the date you collected it. Mold is very likely to grow in plastic bags.

Keep in mind that plants retain their properties for the first year, so marking the container with the date is essential. Alternatively, you can combine it with oil and place it in ice cube trays before freezing them. When you want to use it, simply take it out and let it cook alongside the rest of the food.

Cleavers

Galium Aparine is the scientific name for this substance. They are members of the Rubiaceae plant family and are now considered native to North America, despite having originated in Asia, Africa, and even Europe.

Some people will develop a mild form of dermatitis if they come into contact with cleavers, so wear gloves if you are allergic to them.

How to Collect it.

Cleavers should be harvested early in the spring. Actually, the sooner the better! They'll have some small sticky hooks that can pinch you and, believe it or not, hurt!

How to Keep It.

Allow them to dry naturally before storing them in a paper bag or jars with tight lids in a cool, dry, dark place. You should label the container with the plant's name and the date you collected it. Mold is very likely to grow in plastic bags.

Keep in mind that plants retain their properties for the first year, so marking the container with the date is essential. Alternatively, You can combine it with oil and place it in ice cube trays before freezing them. When you want to use it, simply take it out and let it cook alongside the rest of the food.

Pawpaws

These fruit trees are native to the Americas, and they are related to the cherimoya. If you live in a warm climate, you are likely to come across these small trees. You can eat them raw or blend them into a smoothie!

Its seeds are also very healthy if you boil them and drink the water after it has cooled!

How to Collect it

You will be able to find this type of fruit if you live in Florida or Texas. Harvest them when they begin to turn yellow or orange, not when they are still green, as this color indicates they are not yet ready to be consumed.

How to Keep It

You can store them in the fridge, cut them into small squares and freeze them, or make jam with them. You can also keep the seeds and plant them.

CHAPTER 4

Everything You Need to Know About Edible Wild Plants in

Summer

Oh, summertime! Foragers love this time of year because they can go out into nature and find incredible plants that will not only aid them in their healing journey, but will also provide great nutritional value to their diets.

If you start foraging now, you will see things growing everywhere, but most importantly, you will see food everywhere!

This chapter will educate you on everything there is to know about

Summer edible wild plants:

What You Should Know About Summer Foraging.

All plants will make an appearance when summer arrives. Greens will sprout everywhere, and fruits will become more juice-like. Summer is the season when you won't (and shouldn't) stop, especially if you're into foraging.

You'll have to taste the plants and fruits to decide how you want to eat them, as their flavor changes throughout the season.

Going foraging in the summer is simply amazing and exciting; not only will you have beautiful weather, but you will also be able to learn about and see a variety of edible wild plants.

Types of Edible Wild Plants Available in Summer

Here are some of the edible wild plants you can find and forage for this season.

Blackberries

They are known as Rubus fruticosus and are high in vitamin C and K, providing an immediate energy boost. You could eat them fresh from the bush, or you could make pies, fruit smoothies, or even eat them with yogurt! With this fruit, the possibilities are endless!

Wear gloves if you want to avoid getting the fruit's color on your hands (which happens a lot once you start foraging blackberries all the time!).

Be aware

Blackberries have been shown to lower blood sugar levels, so if you have diabetes, avoid eating the leaves.

How to Collect it.

This delicious fruit is available at the end of spring and beginning of summer, but it will last throughout these seasons.

How to Keep It.

If you want to eat the leaves, you can easily grind or dry them. Alternatively, if you are consuming the fruits, you can store them in the refrigerator.

Black Walnuts

They are also known scientifically as Juglans nigra and are members of the Juglandaceae plant family. Although the entire plant is medicinal, you should only eat the nut meats. Even though these nuts may take longer to process (especially when compared to other types of foraged plants), they will be well worth the wait!

Important note:

The leaves can be made into a tincture or tea. Wear gloves; otherwise, your hands will be stained with the yellow-brown color released by the nuts.

You should avoid using this nut tincture if you are pregnant or breastfeeding, as it may cause serious internal harm.

How to Collect it.

They should be harvested throughout the summer, though I believe they taste better near the end of the season.

How to Keep It.

You could either completely dry them and place them in bags or small containers, or you could make a tea bag and place them in there. You could also store the nuts meat in a container and they will retain their moisture.

Ground Cherries:

These plants will be available throughout the season! Did you also know they are related to tomatoes? They are a fruit that looks like miniature lanterns and can be orange, yellow, or cream in color.

Important note:

If you know how to cook with tomatoes, you can easily cook with ground cherries! They're so similar, in fact, that you can make sauces with ground cherries instead of tomatoes!

Be aware that if the fruit is not ripe, it may be harmful to some people (or even poisonous).

How to Collect it.

They should be harvested throughout the summer, though I believe they taste better near the end of the season. Another thing to keep in mind is that the husk should be brown before harvesting, as this indicates that the fruit is now ripe.

How to Keep It.

You can either store them in the fridge or freeze them after cooking!

Milkweed

They will bloom, and a pink flower will open, becoming extremely fragrant. This plant is very common in North America and is very easy to identify.

Important note:

You can cook the pods like vegetables, but you must boil them twice for at least three minutes each time. When you boil them, make sure to change the water.

How to Collect it.

You should harvest them in mid-summer, but I believe they taste better towards the end of the season, as the flavor will be more intense but still really good.

How to Keep It.

Allow them to dry naturally before storing them in a paper bag or jars with tight lids in a cool, dry, dark place. You should label the container with the plant's name and the date you collected it. Mold is very likely to grow in plastic bags.

Keep in mind that plants retain their properties for the first year, so marking the container with the date is essential. Alternatively, you can combine it with oil and place it in ice cube trays before freezing them. When you want to use it, simply take it out and let it cook alongside the rest of the food.

Plantain

This edible wild plant, scientifically known as Plantago spp., Plantaginaceae, can be found in the spring, though it can be found all year in some areas. They are extremely beneficial plants (Sarfraz, 2017). They are not to be confused with other kinds of plantains (that are from the same family as bananas).

Important note:

Make sure to thoroughly rinse the plantain plants.

How to Collect it.

Plantains are edible, but it is best to harvest them at the beginning of summer if you want to eat them. However, you can eat them all year; just make sure to add some lemon zest to make the plant's flavor less strong.

How to Keep It.

Allow them to dry naturally before storing them in a paper bag or jars with tight lids in a cool, dry, dark place. You should label the container with the plant's name and the date you collected it. Mold is very likely to grow in plastic bags.

Keep in mind that plants retain their properties for the first year, so marking the container with the date is essential.

Cattails

They are wildflowers with an interesting shape! They can be found in most wetlands, usually (but not always) during late spring and early summer. When the cattails reach maturity, their flower turns yellow.

Important note:

Cattails have male and female spikes.

The male is usually at the top, while the female is at the bottom.

Keep in mind that when the cattail flower turns dark brown, it is no longer edible.

How to Collect it.

You should harvest them all summer long. Place your fingers on the swelling at the top of the plant, right in the center of the stalk. If it's soft, they're probably ready to be harvested. If not, leave them for a few days and then return to them. You can collect pollen if you touch them and the pollen is dispersed.

How to Keep It.

Allow them to dry naturally before storing them in a paper bag or jars with tight lids in a cool, dry, dark place. You ought to

Put the plant's name and the date you collected it on the container. Mold is very likely to grow in plastic bags.

Keep in mind that plants retain their properties for the first year, so marking the container with the date is essential.

Horse Balm or Bee Balm?

They are both mint-related. These plants can be found throughout the United States, though they are more likely to be found in prairies or coastal plains.

Important note:

Its leaves can be used to make tea.

How to Collect it.

They should be harvested at the end of the summer. Even though they will appear at the start of the season, they will be too small to eat.

How to Keep It.

Allow them to dry naturally before storing them in a paper bag or jars with tight lids in a cool, dry, dark place. You should label the container with the plant's name and the date you collected it. Mold is very likely to grow in plastic bags.

Keep in mind that plants retain their properties for the first year, so marking the container with the date is essential.

Wild Plums

They belong to the Prunus family. These plants will be found throughout the United States. You'll recognize this fruit by its white flowers, and you can eat it as soon as it's ripe.

Important note:

Its leaves can be used to make tea.

How to Collect it.

You should harvest them all summer long.

Make sure the fruit is ripe so that it can be harvested easily.

How to Keep It.

You could store them in your refrigerator like any other fruit. You could also make some jam or jellies and store them in jars.

CHAPTER 5

Everything You Need to Know About Edible Wild Plants in Fall

The previous season was crucial because it allowed you to solidify your knowledge of edible wild plants. And now you're noticing how the leaves are starting to fall, the colors are changing everywhere, and the food you used to forage is slowly disappearing.

You will be able to forage mushrooms in the fall because they prefer the humidity of the season. However, you will begin to notice new plants that you have not seen in previous seasons.

If you go for a walk in the early fall, you will quickly realize how much edible wild food is still available for foraging. Some people believe that this is the best time to go foraging because the fruits are already ripening and the nuts are usually on the ground. On the other hand, mushrooms are more likely to be found!

You learned how to forage, what to look for, and how to consume and preserve what you foraged over the last two seasons. If you pay close attention this season, you may notice new edible wild plants that you have never seen before.

What You Should Know About Fall Foraging

When fall arrives, all plants must make a decision: do they go dormant, die, or continue to grow?

You'll have to taste the plants and fruits to decide how you want to eat them, as their flavor will change throughout the season. You may need to be cautious at times; otherwise, your plants or fruits may be lost because they mature far too quickly.

Types of Edible Wild Plants Available In Fall

Let's take a look at what you might be able to forage this season.

Beech Nuts

Fagus sylvatica is the scientific name for this tree. They are edible wild nuts that are frequently used to feed pigs due to their nutritional value, despite the fact that they are very small, so you would have to consume a lot to feel full! Before attempting to consume it, you must scrape the entire outer and thicker skin. In fact, you must see the small seed because it contains the nut!

You should avoid eating a lot of beech nuts because they contain tannins and other types of alkaloids that can cause allergic reactions.

How to Collect it.

All you have to do is pick them up off the ground! You can roast them in the oven if you want; this will soften the shells and make them easier to peel. They usually fall between mid-September and the beginning of November.

How to Keep It.

They can be placed in a hermetic container. If not, make a sauce or pesto with them and freeze it.

Hop

Humulus lupulus is the scientific name for this plant. This type of plant can be found climbing along various hedgerows. If you want, you can eat the entire plant. They are medicinal plants with a high antioxidant content (Knez Hrni, 2019).

How to Collect it.

It should be harvested in the early or mid-fall.

How to Keep It.

Allow them to dry naturally before storing them in a paper bag or jars with tight lids in a cool, dry, dark place. You should label the container with the plant's name and the date you collected it. Mold is very likely to grow in plastic bags.

Keep in mind that plants retain their properties for the first year, so marking the container with the date is essential. Alternatively, you can combine it with oil and place it in ice cube trays before freezing them. When you want to use it, simply take it out and let it cook alongside the rest of the food.

Persimmons

These are native to the southeast region of the United States, so you can find them there.

How to Collect it.

You must ensure that the fruit is soft and ripe; otherwise, the flavor may be unpleasant. Persimmons are bitter and sometimes sour! Harvesting should be delayed until the end of the fall.

How to Keep It.

You could store them in the fridge or make jelly or jam to preserve the fruit.

The Chicory Root

It's worth noting that if you eat chicory leaves in the fall, they'll probably be too bitter and won't taste as good. However, you could eat the roots and drink them like coffee! Alternatively, you can eat the roots, which will fill you up (Fouré, 2018)!

Important note:

You can also drink chicory root tea. Just make sure to boil them first.

How to Collect it.

Take the roots out of the soil. Chicory roots can be harvested throughout the season.

How to Keep It.

You could either completely dry them and place them in bags or small containers, or you could make a tea bag and place them in there.

Violets

If you want to look for violets, this is the time to do it. They're fantastic for making vinegar or adding to tea!

Important note:

Violet leaves can also be used to make syrup. They have numerous medicinal properties.

How to Collect it.

Violets can be harvested all through the fall. In fact, because they are frost-hardy, you can do so even in the dead of winter.

How to Keep It.

Allow them to dry naturally before storing them in a paper bag or jars with tight lids in a cool, dry, dark place. You should label the container with the plant's name and the date you collected it. Mold is very likely to grow in plastic bags.

Keep in mind that plants retain their properties for the first year, so marking the container with the date is essential.

Goldenrod

People usually claim to be allergic to goldenrods, even though this type of yellow flower is also very medicinal!

How to Collect it.

It can be harvested all through the fall.

How to Keep It.

Allow them to dry naturally before storing them in a paper bag or jars with tight lids in a cool, dry, dark place. You should label the container with the plant's name and the date you collected it. Mold is very likely to grow in plastic bags.

Keep in mind that plants retain their properties for the first year, so marking the container with the date is essential.

Chinese Chestnut

They are members of the Fagaceae plant and nut family and are also known as Castanea mollissima. They should not be consumed raw; instead, they should be cooked.

Be aware that other nuts look similar to Chinese chestnuts but are poisonous. Before you consume it, make sure you can tell the difference.

How to Collect it.

Always keep your head down! Especially if you happen to be in the southern Appalachians in the middle of autumn, when you should be harvesting these nuts.

How to Keep It.

You could prepare them and freeze them. You could also use it to make nut butter and keep it in the fridge.

Sweet Chestnuts

As you can see, autumn is the ideal season for all kinds of nuts! Even though squirrels adore them (and probably eat the majority of them), you can still find some by looking down whenever you go for a walk.

Be aware:

Some people are allergic to nuts; eat only a couple at first to see how your body reacts.

How to collect it

This season is ideal for harvesting sweet chestnuts.

How to Keep It.

Make a pesto sauce or nut butter and store it in the refrigerator. You could also store them in hermetic containers.

Autumn or Fall Olives

Although the name implies that they are olives, they are not! What a jumble of names! This fruit is a berry, and it grows on shrubs that have the potential to grow into full-sized trees. In the central and eastern United States, they are considered invasive species.

Important note: They must be fully ripe before being consumed; therefore, wrap two fingers around them and feel how it feels; if it is too hard, they are not edible yet.

Be aware that if they are not fully ripe, they can be astringent.

How to Collect it.

You can harvest them all season long.

How to Keep It.

You have the option of making jelly, cookies, or pies. Alternatively, you can store them in the refrigerator for a couple of weeks.

Acorns

As you can see, there will be a wide variety of nuts available in the fall, even in the wilderness! Acorns, on the other hand, will not be found at your local supermarket; apparently, they do not like to sell them! To be honest, this is fantastic news for us, foragers.

If you live near mature oak trees, take a walk beneath them; you will most likely find these acorns. They are so easy to recognize that you won't even have to worry about eating the wrong nut. And they have many nutritional benefits; for example, they are high in calories and fat, which are both really good when you think about it, especially if a person has to rely on these nuts while foraging.

Important note:

Although they are very healthy, you should not eat them raw because acorns contain tannins, which make them poisonous and dangerous to eat in their natural state (as do many other types of nuts).

How to Collect it.

When you're ready to harvest acorns, make sure you have plenty of water nearby so you can thoroughly rinse them. Ideally, you should repeat this process more than five times to ensure that the acorn no longer has a bitter taste.

How to Keep It.

Acorns can be used to make nut butter or simply stored in a hermetic container in your pantry.

CHAPTER 6

Everything You Need to Know About Edible Wild Plants in Winter

Winter, oh winter. One of the most difficult seasons for foragers. Depending on where you live, you will most likely have a difficult time finding food to forage in your area.

Do not, however, give up! In the dead of winter, it's not impossible to find a nutritious, healthy, and delicious plant. You simply need to keep your eyes open and observe more.

Some people dread winter because it is not only extremely cold in some areas, but it also means that the flu season has only just begun! However, with your newfound foraging knowledge, you can easily dismiss these fears of becoming ill, because the plants you find can be your medicine...or, better yet, you can use them to prevent illness.

This chapter will educate you on everything there is to know about

Winter edible wild plants

What You Should Know About Winter Foraging.

Winter is often regarded as a difficult season because fall has already passed, but spring is still a few months away. There aren't many of our "usual" fruits or plants growing outside, but there are plenty of berries and other types of fruits that will make winter foraging a memorable experience.

Of course, it all depends on where you live. However, foraging during this season should not be regarded as completely difficult or impossible.

Types of Edible Wild Plants Available This Season

Let's take a look at what you might be able to forage this season.

Miner's Lettuce

Claytonia perfoliate is another name for it. They look like chickweed, but if you look closely, you can tell the difference. Miner's lettuce, for example, has rounder leaves, whereas chickweed has oval leaves.

How to Collect it.

You can harvest them all season because they thrive in cooler temperatures.

How to Keep It.

Allow them to dry naturally before storing them in a paper bag or jars with tight lids in a cool, dry, dark place. You should label the container with the plant's name and the date you collected it. Mold is very likely to grow in plastic bags.

Keep in mind that plants retain their properties for the first year, so marking the container with the date is essential. Alternatively, you can combine it with oil and place it in ice cube trays before freezing them. When you want to use it, simply take it out and let it cook alongside the rest of the food.

Wild Violet

They are both very medicinal plants that you can easily find throughout the United States during winter, especially if you live in an area where winters are not harsh. They are scientifically known as viola sororia or viola odorata.

Important note: You can bake with wild violets or make vinegar with them!

How to Collect it.

If you live in a warm climate, you can harvest them all season.

How to Keep It.

You have the option of making jelly, cookies, or pies. Alternatively, you can store them in the refrigerator for a couple of weeks.

Mullein

Verbascum Thapsus is the scientific name for this plant. If you've ever seen mullein, I'm sure you've mentioned its leaf! They have a very interesting appearance! Some people call it "cowboy's toilet paper," but I wouldn't use it as a substitute for toilet paper when you're out in the wilderness because it has very small hairs that can irritate your skin. But did you know that mulleins are also high in nutritional value?

How to Collect it.

You can harvest them all season long, especially if you live in a dry state like the United States.

How to Keep It.

It can be dried and ground. Some people smoke it after mixing it with tobacco.

Barberry

Many people will notice a resemblance between barberries and wild roses because they are similar in appearance. Barberries, on the other hand, have an oval shape and redder fruits than wild roses. If you live on the east coast of the United States, you will notice this fruit in the winter.

Important note: Barberries are extremely beneficial to your health. They contain berberine, which makes you feel better as soon as you consume them (Imenshahidi, 2019.).

Keep in mind that eating the seeds may cause indigestion.

How to Collect it.

You can harvest them all season long.

How to Keep It.

You have the option of making jelly, cookies, or pies. Alternatively, you can store them in the refrigerator for a couple of weeks.

Hickory Nuts

They taste very similar to pecans, albeit in a wild form of the former! Consider gathering a few of these nuts if you want to add more good calories to your diet, especially if you go foraging.

Be aware that some hickory nuts can be extremely bitter when consumed. They are not poisonous but after just one bite,

You should probably put it away!

How to Collect it.

You can harvest them all season long.

How to Keep It.

You have the option of making jelly, cookies, or pies. Alternatively, you can store them in the refrigerator for a couple of weeks.

Alexanders

This plant, scientifically known as Smyrnium olusatrum, is completely edible. Because it tastes similar to parsley, you can use it in salads, soups, meats, stews, and anything else you're cooking!

How to Collect it.

You can harvest them all season long.

How to Keep It.

Allow them to dry naturally before storing them in a paper bag or jars with tight lids in a cool, dry, dark place. You should label the container with the plant's name and the date you collected it. Mold is very likely to grow in plastic bags.

Keep in mind that plants retain their properties for the first year, so marking the container with the date is essential.

Wild Cranberries

If you live in the Northeastern United States, you are likely to come across wild cranberries!

How to Collect it.

You can harvest them all season because they can withstand harsh weather conditions.

How to Keep It.

You have the option of making jelly, cookies, or pies. Alternatively, you can store them in the refrigerator for a couple of weeks.

Cattails

They are wildflowers with an interesting shape! They can be found in most wetlands, usually (but not always) in late winter, spring, and early summer. When the cattails reach maturity, their flower turns yellow.

Important note: Cattails have male and female spikes.

The male is usually at the top, while the female is at the bottom.

Keep in mind that when the cattail flower turns dark brown, it is no longer edible.

How to Collect it.

You should harvest them throughout the summer, but if you live in a very warm area, you may be able to find some cattails in the winter. Place your fingers on the swelling at the top of the plant, right in the center of the stalk. If it's soft, they're probably ready to be harvested. If not, leave them for a few days and then return to them. You can collect pollen if you touch them and the pollen is dispersed.

How to Keep It.

You could either completely dry them and place them in bags or small containers, or you could make a tea bag and place them in there.

CHAPTER 7

Foraging Herbs, Spices and Flowers

Foraging is the process of looking for, identifying, harvesting, and storing edible wild plants. It is not only a healthy activity, but it is also a pleasurable one, especially once you begin cooking with all of the herbs, flowers, and spices you have foraged throughout the year.

Aromatic plants (or herbs) can be used in the kitchen to enhance the flavor, aroma, and color of meals, as well as to make them more appealing in some cases.

However, you can prepare an infusion to drink after the meal or delight your palate throughout the day. There are wild herbs for every taste, whether it's mint or chamomile tea, lemon or lemon balm.

How to properly store spices, flowers, and herbs.

Allow them to dry naturally before storing them in a paper bag or jars with tight lids in a cool, dry, dark place.

You should label the container with the plant's name and the date you collected it.

Mold is very likely to grow in plastic bags.

Keep in mind that plants retain their properties for the first year, so marking the container with the date is essential.

Alternatively, you can combine them with oil, place them in ice cube trays, and freeze them. When you want to use it, simply take it out and let it cook alongside the rest of the food.

Herbs, Flowers, and Spices You Can Forage All Year Here are some of the most common herbs, spices, and flowers you can forage all year.

Hairy Bittercress

Cardamine hirsute is another name for it. This annual herb has a strong flavor, but some gardeners consider it a weed because it spreads so quickly.

Important note: To find the Hairy bittercress herbs, you must closely observe nature because they will hide within a compact rosette that will stay close to the soil.

How to Collect it.

Despite being an annual herb, you can harvest the majority of it throughout the season.

How to Keep It.

You can use it to make pesto and store it in the fridge or freezer.

Wintergreen

This plant is similar to blueberries, though it is found in fewer places than the plant mentioned above. They now have

Horizontal rhizomes that could grow to be quite large, especially if no one has ever taken that plant before and it has been left to grow wild.

Important note: When foraging for this plant, look for the little black dots that contain resin. They are usually found beneath the leaves; this ensures that you have foraged the correct herb.

How to Collect it.

They should be harvested throughout the summer, though I believe they taste better near the end of the season.

Yarrow

Achillea millefolium is the scientific name for this plant. They can be found almost anywhere! It's a wild plant that helps humans regulate their blood pressure; it's frequently used as a wound-healing herb, which means it's very effective at preventing blood clots.

Important note: The leaves can also be used in salads or soups. I also made Yarrow's lasagna, which was delicious!

How to Collect it.

They should be harvested throughout the spring.

Lemon Balm

Melissa officinalis is the scientific name for this plant. They are members of the Lamiaceae plant family. It is a simple herb that you can forage if you need an antiviral and digestive ally, as it contains many beneficial properties that will boost your immune system.

How to Collect it.

Lemon balm can be harvested all year in some warmer regions of the United States. If you live in a cold climate, however, you will most likely find this herb throughout the spring.

Elderberries

Elderberries are a shrub or small perennial tree found in many parts of the United States that are related to the Adoxaceae plant family.

Elderberries will produce small white flowers near the end of spring, and the berries will be visible only after they appear.

Important note:

If you eat fresh elderberries, you will quickly notice that the flavor is very strong. You could easily dry them to make the flavor more palatable.

How to Collect it.

You can harvest them throughout the summer, but I believe they taste best at the start of the season. After the flowers appear, rub the stems with your fingers and then remove the berries from the plant.

Wild Rose

Rosa spp. is a plant species in the Rosaceae family. These wild roses are among the oldest plants on the planet, having existed for thousands of years.

Important note: The entire plant is edible.

How to Collect it.

Wild roses can be found all over the United States. They are typically found from late spring to late fall.

Honey Balm

Monarda spp. is the scientific name for this plant. This herb is related to mints because it comes from the Lamiaceae plant family! They are frequently regarded as invasive weeds due to their ability to grow and spread throughout the soil.

How to Collect it. Harvest them when they have flowered; this indicates that the herb is ready to be consumed.

Red Clovers

Clovers are members of the pea family, did you know? There are many different types of clovers, but this one in particular can be found all summer.

Important note: You can eat them raw or cook with them in salads or other dishes.

How to Collect it.

You should harvest them throughout the summer, but make sure the flower heads are fully opened and before they turn brown.

Rosemary

Rosmarinus officinalis is the scientific name for rosemary. This herb is a favorite in our kitchens! But did you know that this is one of the simplest herbs to forage for? Particularly if you live in a hot state! It is also excellent medicine for people (Nieto, 2018).

Important note: Because this herb is so versatile, it can be used to cook meat as well as make an infusion.

How to Collect it.

Always choose the largest plants because the smaller ones are sometimes too weak to harvest. This herb will become available at the beginning of spring.

Sage

Salvia officinalis is the scientific name for this plant. This is yet another herb that can be found almost anywhere! Particularly if you live in a hot state!

Important note: Because this herb is so versatile, it can be used to cook stews as well as make an infusion.

How to Collect it.

Always choose the largest plants because the smaller ones are sometimes too weak to harvest. This herb will be available beginning in the early summer.

Peppermint

Mentha x Piperita is the scientific name for this plant. This herb is one of several types of herbs in the Mint family. They are plants of the Lamiaceae family. It is classified as an invasive weed due to its rapid spread. It is a herb that is easily identified due to its strong fragrance.

Important note: Peppermint has numerous medicinal properties. It can cause sore throats, but it can also help with digestion.

How to Collect it.

Always choose the largest plants because the smaller ones are sometimes too weak to harvest. This herb will be available beginning in the early summer.

Other Flowers You Should Look for

Comfrey: Although it is commonly regarded as a weed, these purple flowers are very popular among foragers due to their delicious flavor!

Wild Coriander: If you want to add a new flavor and scent to your food, go foraging for wild coriander.

This herb has a wild form that, in my opinion, tastes even better than regular coriander!

You will gradually learn which flowers to forage for and where to look for them. You will also realize how amazing this new foraging lifestyle is, especially when you consider the environmental aspect of using flowers to make tea or eat!

You will not only save money by not buying store-bought teas, but you will also be able to solve many health problems by finding in nature what you need to help you maintain your health or correct something that is wrong.

I know it may seem intimidating at first, especially because foraging doesn't always leave much room for error, but please try to persevere! I can assure you that the experiments you conduct with edible wild plants will result in new discoveries and reveal new information about your health. And, because you will learn more about nature, you will become more conscious of how you forage and live your life. But, most importantly, have fun discovering what your foraging activities can provide for you!

CHAPTER 8

Identification of Poisonous Wild Plants

Any experienced forager will agree on one point: when we first started out on this journey, we were easily carried away whenever we went out to harvest our food. It's as if we were always looking for food, and sometimes we made silly mistakes (like eating the root even though it's not edible), but other times we could have seriously injured ourselves or others if we hadn't been careful enough.

Going foraging requires caution because you will be identifying many poisonous wild plants that are not edible. In fact, the majority of the plants (up to 93% or more) are not edible. So, if you think about it, whenever you go foraging, you will almost certainly see more non-edible plants than edible plants.

Furthermore, if you are an experienced forager accompanying a new forager, you must definitely pass this knowledge on to them, as it is easy to forget when we are new to this game. We'd like to see how everything tastes in our casserole, or we'd like to try new skin balms!

In fact, I would always advise people to work in pairs or groups, with each group bringing a knowledgeable person who is knowledgeable about wild edibles...

The more the better!

Otherwise, we are always at risk, especially if we are confused and harvest a plant that looks similar to the edible ones, only to discover that it is not edible at all!

This chapter will assist you in correctly identifying the poisonous, non-edible wild plants that you must avoid at all costs:

Avoid Using These Plants:

- If you come across these plants and are unsure whether or not you can eat them, I recommend taking a second look.
- If the plants produce legumes but you can't identify the plant, don't eat them.
- If the plants have a white sap, avoid them because it could be toxic.
- If the plants are very spikey or sharp, don't eat them (or you'll end up with spikes in your tongue!). Although some plants can be eaten if thoroughly cooked. If you notice a dying plant, do not even touch it! Nature's processes must be respected.

Symptoms That a Plant Is Poisonous

Some indicators can help you determine whether or not to avoid certain plants. If you're unsure and see one of these signs, DON'T TAKE THE CHANCE! Avoid plants that exhibit the following characteristics: Spines or thorns Bitter flavor Sap with a soapy taste or that is milky or discolored Plant or growth pattern with three leaves (unless they are clovers) Seeds or beans found within pods Anything that resembles dill, parsley, or carrots, as they may be poisonous! It has an almond scent.

When foraging, it is critical to avoid the aforementioned characteristics because they may indicate that the plants you are looking at are poisonous, and sometimes extremely poisonous!

Read this book as many times as necessary. Still, if you learn to safely identify the previously described edible wild plants and ignore these poisonous look-alikes, your foraging trip should be a success!

Remember that this is an investment because this knowledge could literally save your life if you were ever in a difficult survival situation.

What should you avoid!? Why not avoid them?

You must ensure that whatever you are about to consume or apply (to your skin as a lotion or balm) is edible or can be used topically. Otherwise, you risk having an allergic reaction, food poisoning, or even more serious problems down the road.

I'm not trying to scare you away from foraging; rather, I'm attempting to do the opposite. But I do want you to be completely honest and clear whenever you are about to identify a new plant because they have the potential to change your future in an instant!

Even if you are certain about the plant in front of you, you should take a small bite first. When you're certain it's safe, you can forage it completely and take it home to make whatever dishes you want!

Not only should you be able to identify the plant correctly, but you should also be able to correctly identify that it is an edible wild plant.

You Should Avoid Poisonous Plants

When foraging, you must ensure that you are fully prepared to identify the appropriate plants for consumption. If you want to successfully harvest your food, you must also prioritize your own safety and protection. As a result, identifying non-edible wild plants is essential whenever you begin foraging. You cannot make any mistakes, even if they may occur at some point.

Earth Smoke

Fumaria officinalis is the scientific name for this lovely plant. This plant can be found all over North America. It belongs to the poppy family, and while it is medicinal, it can also be poisonous if consumed.

The Lily of the Valley

This plant, scientifically known as Convallaria majalis, should be handled with extreme caution because it is extremely poisonous! The worst part is that many people mistake this plant for wild onions, wild garlic, wild leeks, or ramsons. Even though they have some similarities, the one tip I can give you that works every time is this: if you think "wild onion or wild garlic" are the same plants and they aren't lily of the valley, then they must have a strong odor.

They should, in fact, smell like garlic and onions! If the plant you're about to forage looks like garlic and onions but doesn't smell like them, you're looking at lily of the valley.

Glorybower Harlequin

Clerodendrum trichotomum is the scientific name for this plant. If you ever come across one of these plants, you will not only be extremely fortunate but you will be astounded by their beauty.

This plant has a distinct shape and color scheme. It has bright blue berries that are surrounded by a pink and red structure known as a calyx. I've never seen anything like this before, and I've been foraging for a long time.

However, as much as I would like to take it home, I am aware that the seeds and even some plant parts are highly poisonous if consumed. Even touching them can result in severe skin rashes or reactions. Don't even think about touching it!

Rattlebox

Crotalaria spectabilis is the scientific name for this plant. This plate features bright yellow flowers that appear so innocent that you almost want to harvest them! But don't be taken in! They are completely toxic to both humans and animals, and all of the plants are poisonous! They were commonly found in the southeastern United States.

Honeyvine

Cynanchum laeve is another name for this plant. This is a highly poisonous plant that is easily confused with the milkweed vine. However, the sap released by the honey vine may cause permanent damage to your eyes and mucus membranes. It is not recommended to even touch this plant, let alone consume it, as it may prevent your heart from pumping blood! Consider how powerful this plant is!

It is native to the eastern United States and can be found throughout the region.

Mulberry Weed

Fatoua villosa is another name for this plant. It is also known as hairy crab weed. It's a very invasive plant that grows in the Mississippi area. If you touch the leaves or stems, it can cause itching.

Mexican Poppy

Argemone Mexicana is another name for it. This lovely plant can have either yellow or white flowers. It is easily identified due to its spiny leaves. It can be found throughout the United States, but it is more popular in the east.

Because it has medicinal properties, some people will use it in herbal medicine. If you eat them, however, they are extremely poisonous.

Tahitian Wedding Veil

Gibasis geniculata is the scientific name for this plant. Because it is so similar to the spiderwort plant, foragers frequently confuse the two. The spiderwort, on the other hand, is edible, whereas the Tahitian bridal veil is extremely poisonous to cats, dogs, and humans.

Privet Waxy

Also known as Glossy privet or, more scientifically, Ligustrum lucidum. Although this tree is native to China, it can be found in many parts of the United States, including Texas, Arizona, and California.

Maryland. It has many beneficial medicinal properties; however, its tiny fruits are poisonous!

Spreading Lupine

It is scientifically known as Lupinus diffusus and is colloquially known as Oak Ridge lupine. It is native to dry climates throughout the United States, primarily in the southeastern region. Its seeds are extremely poisonous, even though it is popular as an ornamental plant due to its beautiful purple flowers.

The Castor Bean

Ricinus communis is another name for Ricinus communis. This type of plant grows in tropical and warm climates, and it is the source of castor oil, which is generally safe to consume. This plant, however, produces seeds that are lethal if consumed raw. I've never tried them cooked, but I wouldn't do it because they contain ricin!

Wavyleaf Basket Grass

Oplismenus hirtellus ssp. Undulatifolius is the scientific name for this plant. Try saying it out loud! This plant is not native to the United States, but it is now common in the southern states.

Wavyleaf basket grass is extremely toxic to humans.

The Giant Hogweed

Heracleum mantegazzianum is the scientific name for this plant. This plant is as large as its name suggests! It can grow up to 15 feet tall and is not only toxic, but also one of nature's most dangerous and toxic plants.

The Giant Hogweed produces sap that causes any skin to swell and causes blisters to form on the surface. Even if you only lightly touch it, it can cause permanent scarring.

It may also cause temporary or permanent blindness, so avoid touching it at all costs! Unfortunately, foragers have occasionally touched this plant; if this is the case, thoroughly wash the affected area and remove it from the sunlight for a couple of days, if not longer. And see your doctor right away!

The Giant Hogweed is found in the Northeastern United States. It grows from Maine all the way to Virginia, demonstrating how easily they spread.

Mistletoe

Phoradendron serotinum is the scientific name for this plant. Many people will not believe this plant is toxic because its white berries are commonly seen in many homes during the Christmas season. However, it is a parasitic evergreen plant that forms a vine and, if eaten, can cause immediate harm.

If you consume Mistletoe, you may experience diarrhea, vomiting, nausea, and even seizures! As a result, keep it away from children and small animals!

Butterweed

Senecio glabellus is the scientific name for this species. It is only found in North and Central America. It has yellow seeds and a yellow flower, and it looks so much like wild mustard that people often confuse the two. Butterweed, on the other hand, is easily identified because its leaves are not sandpapery.

Scarlet Sage

Also known as Salvia cocinnea. It is native to Texas and can be found as far south as the Southern Hemisphere. It has a strong aroma comparable to sage This plant should not be eaten because it can cause serious damage to your intestines. It adds beauty to any garden but does not consume it!

Horse Nettle

It is also known by its scientific name, Solanum. It is widely available throughout the United States. This plant will produce a highly toxic fruit, especially when it is green, so avoid eating it!

Four O'Clock Plant

This is a case of "these flowers look so delicate, they can't be harmful, so I'll grab some and eat them," when you should be running away from them! They will kill any pest that comes near them, and their flower is poisonous to both animals and humans! So, please keep children and pets away from it!

Keep These Statements in Mind

Do not eat a plant unless you are absolutely certain it is safe. You could face serious problems if you eat a poisonous plant.

Even if you believe a plant is (or isn't) poisonous, cross-reference it as many times as possible; many plants are edible, many are not, and they all look similar. This is not the time to make any mistakes! If you go foraging with someone who knows more than you, you should always consult with them about the plants you're about to forage. You must properly store the plants after foraging them; otherwise, they will become damaged quickly or even moldy!

CHAPTER 9

Excellent Guidelines to Follow When Foraging Edible Wild Plants

Even though more foragers are appearing all over the world, many people still regard foraging for their own food as a mystery. Furthermore, while edible wild plants vary around the world, the basic principle behind foraging remains the same: you are looking for nutritious food that is free, organic, and healthy!

This sustainable method not only makes sense, but it also begs the question, "Why aren't we all doing it?" Why hasn't it become a common technique for all gardeners, farmers, and people in general all over the world, rather than an illegal activity in many places?

The truth is that foraging for edible wild plants has recently gained popularity as more people realize how much better their health improves when they ditch processed foods and begin eating a more sustainable and green diet.

This does not necessarily imply that people must follow a vegetarian diet, as many of these wild plants taste delicious when combined with meat. However, people will continue to go foraging because they see the benefits firsthand.

We now know that the healthier a person is, the more vigorous and healthy its surrounding areas and ecosystems are, because we are in touch with our roots, with the plants that surround us. We're starting to figure out which edible wild plants are good for us!

Here are some great tips to keep in mind when foraging edible wild plants:

Our top priority is the environment.

We must not only care for the environment in which we live, but we must also be aware of it because that is where the plants grow. If the environment (which includes the soil, air, water, and other plants) is damaged or polluted, we can either stop foraging there or try to improve it. It all depends on your knowledge, experience, willingness to help, and dedication.

If you see a plant that is surrounded by polluted water from a highway (or other nearby areas), that water could contain gasoline or other polluting agents from the road. As a result, the plant you were admiring is no longer edible.

The environment will also provide us with numerous clues about the plants that can be found there. For example, the plant's surroundings may aid in determining the plant's requirements.

If you notice a plant with tilted and sad leaves and realize it is getting too much sun, you now know that this plant will thrive best if it is placed in a shaded area. You could either relocate it or leave it where it is; in either case, you should not forage that particular plant.

Ideally, the area where you go foraging should be free of chemicals and pollution; I know identifying pollutants can be difficult; however, many visible signs will tell you if the area is unhealthy. Consider the following warning signs: If the water is dirty or smells strange, it is likely polluted. If you notice that all of the plants are unhealthy or appear to be dying, there is most likely something in the air. If there are any dead animals nearby, something is clearly wrong with this environment. The environment is polluted if no new plants are growing.

What if you are unable to identify the plant?

If you can't identify the plant (because you don't know where else to look for information, or because you think it's one plant and another person thinks it's another), and you're in a tough situation where you need to eat the plant to survive, I can only recommend a skin test.

You won't be able to eat the plant right away, but you'll know if your body is reacting negatively to it. Do not eat the plant if your tongue feels like it's on fire or if it goes completely numb!

If you have any doubts, don't eat those plants; doubts are usually a warning signal from our instincts. So, follow your instincts and avoid eating the plant! It is preferable to go hungry than to poison yourself by eating an inedible wild plant. Obviously, this is not an ideal situation, but if you are unsure whether the plant is edible or not, and there is no way to find out, I would advise you to leave the plant alone.

Tips for Beginning Foragers

Begin slowly. I know it's impossible to learn everything all at once, so why don't you try to learn slowly? There are numerous edible and inedible plants. There are also more plainly dangerous and poisonous plants. Choose one or two plants to study before moving on. For instance, try to learn three to five plants per month. Try to look for them every time you go foraging. Learn an extra couple as soon as you're comfortable with those! We may become concerned at times because, according to our knowledge, there should be a certain type of plant in spring... However, we haven't seen it at all! This is Mother Nature telling us that climate change is real and that things are happening that are changing all of the ecosystems on the planet. You can understand this and try to be more sustainable by only using what you have available to you. We are constantly learning! Indeed, foragers never stop learning. You might even be a farmer, but once you enter the world of foraging, you will discover many new things.

Read books, download apps, and try to converse with more experienced foragers! You should do everything possible to increase your understanding of this subject. As foragers, we are constantly training our eyes to see beyond what nature shows us. Sometimes we look behind large rocks; other times, we go to difficult-to-reach places because we know there is a great source of protein in that plant or because we have seen many plants of an invasive species and are attempting to control it. When foraging, get comfortable. This includes not only wearing comfortable clothes and shoes but also bringing foraging equipment that is comfortable enough to allow your plants to breathe. In other words, invest in breathable sacks that will protect your plants rather than using plastic bags, which will most likely kill them! Examine each plant for bugs or insects. I know they're high in protein, but I'm sure you don't want to eat them every day! Even if you are foraging for edible wild plants in healthy environments (or are attempting to do so), you will still need to wash your foraged plants before eating them.

You ingest them. A ladybug (or dirt) in a salad doesn't sound particularly appetizing! Do not become overconfident. This is for everyone, whether you are a new or experienced forager. We sometimes go out and forage for food, thinking we're on top of the world because we're getting highly nutritious food for free! I understand; it's very impressive! However, we must remain cautious. We can't be too sure because we have to be careful about what we eat. Even if we have eaten the same plant a thousand times, we never know how our bodies will react. Don't get me wrong: this could also happen with store-bought vegetables and fruits! Your body may wake up one day and say, "I'm not into this anymore!" You should never, ever, ever, ever leave a trace wherever you go. In other words, no one should ever suspect you've been foraging in that location. Not because it is illegal, but because you respect mother earth so much that you do not leave any trash behind, nor do you harm any plants or ecosystems. You are not taking anything that is either rare or protected. Go after the foreigners! Of course, this refers to non-native plants. If you think about it, if you go to an area that is overrun with non-native plants, they are very likely to compete with native plants for survival nutrients. This could also indicate that native plants are struggling to feed themselves and provide nutrients to those who eat or rely on them for survival. If you go foraging and only take nonnative plant species, you are combating invasion and may be saving another environment and ecosystem! Be wary of pesticides, herbicides, and other man-made "aids." You do not want to consume something that has been contaminated sprayed with harmful chemicals that will most likely affect your body, mind, and, ultimately, soul This may appear drastic to some, but if you forage, you are also aware of how many chemicals contaminate fruits and vegetables. This is a common practice in modern agriculture. Going foraging requires you to break free from this cycle and be as organic as possible. Have a good time! What's the point of going foraging if you're not having fun? Going foraging for food should also include going foraging for fun! In fact, I believe that if you go foraging when you are tired or grumpy, you will not be able to find all of the plants you were expecting or wishing for. On the other hand, if you go foraging and you're excited because you're about to do something you enjoy, that's fantastic! Nature will also show up in so many different ways that you won't believe how much you were able to forage. Make a point of carefully observing nature and writing down your observations; this will save you a lot of time in the future, especially if your memory isn't that great. I always bring a notepad and a pen with me when I go foraging in new places. I don't want to forget anything, so I know that writing things down, even if it's just one word, will come in handy later. Did you know that aromatic and medicinal plants contribute to an increase in the biodiversity that your garden can have if you start an organic garden?

They will also help you fight crop pests and make your garden look like a natural system in balance where vegetables, flowers, aromatic herbs, and wild weeds coexist peacefully.

Remembering is essential when foraging for edible wild plants.

Before we continue learning about foraging and what types of edible wild plants you may be able to consume, let's think about this scenario first:

Assume it's your birthday, and your parents are throwing a party in your honor at their home. You've invited all of your family and friends, so you know it'll be a fantastic party!

You walk towards your parents' house, and they all express surprise at your presence, and you are overjoyed to be there. Then, as you're about to greet everyone who came to your party, you realize you've forgotten everyone's name. In fact, you've forgotten your own name.

You can't believe it; it all seems too strange to you. So you start feeling strange and uneasy, and you start questioning everyone to find out who they are. You recognize their faces but have forgotten their names! Until you realize it's all a dream and your birthday isn't for another six months!

Why am I telling you this right now? When you think about it, a similar thing happens when you plan to go foraging in nature. You might recognize some of the plants (or none of them), but aside from their physical appearance, you don't know much about them.

This is why I always tell new foragers this analogy because it is a general rule of thumb. Learn the names of edible wild plants and their relatives; otherwise, your foraging experience may be tainted by mistakes you make when you think a certain plant is something but it is actually a completely different plant.

It would be fantastic and extremely useful if you could learn the names of the herbs, plants, fruits, vegetables, and even mushrooms or trees that you come across are in your area, especially if you intend to consume them.

Of course, this will take some time, but it is a worthwhile investment if you are serious about foraging for edible wild plants. You could easily learn five to ten plants each time you go foraging, and believe it or not, this could save your life in the future!

Tips for Elderly Foragers

Have you ever considered taking someone foraging? Have you ever considered becoming someone else's mentor? This could be beneficial to you in a variety of ways because you will be passing on your knowledge to someone else. You will share a pleasant moment in nature with another person, and you will also have a backup in case you are unsure whether a wild plant is edible. Have you ever considered starting a garden? But, in particular, a garden in which only edible wild plants are allowed to grow? Where you are not afraid of weeds...in fact, you welcome weeds to come in so you can eat them!? Have you ever considered foraging for a living? This may not seem ideal to some but consider it. If you have your own space and garden and plenty of wild plants, why not harvest them and make a living off of them? A good friend of mine, for example, makes a variety of pesto sauces from edible wild plants. She makes a living from something that few people consider harvesting, but many of those same people will buy her pesto sauces! You can easily make this if you have a lot of plantains, wild garlic, and other types of wild plants on hand. Obviously, I don't recommend doing this if you don't have space and go foraging in a public area, as you'll need to consider sustainability. But

If you have your own garden or an area to forage from, this is an excellent side job.

If you are a forager and want to start your own garden (or even improve the soil conditions of your existing garden), did you know that you can help it by harvesting some edible wild plants?

Every particle of soil is alive, with millions (if not billions!) of organisms and microorganisms constantly working to produce the nutrients that plants require.

When it comes to enriching the soil in your gardens, you may be surprised to learn that, contrary to popular belief, neither a chemical nor an organic fertilizer is required. Nature will respond to the stimulus of growing something that will eventually enrich the soil if you choose some edible wild plants wisely.

Plants will supply the necessary nutrients NPK, which stands for Nitrogen, Phosphorus, and Potassium. They will also provide plenty of vitamins and minerals to the soil, which is essential for its survival.

Having good soil also means your plants will grow significantly faster, be healthier, and produce that is good, tasty, and of high quality. This means that if you have a garden, you may benefit from doing some work to protect and enrich your soil, which will eventually allow edible wild plants into your garden.

CHAPTER 10

Medicinal Potentials Of Foraged Edible Wild Plants

When it comes to medicinal plants, it is critical to understand each plant, which part is used, how it is prepared, and how much you should use.

Medicinal plants are commonly used in teas for flavor, care, or because it is better for our health. There are wild herbs for every taste, whether you like mint or chamomile tea, lemon or lemon balm, or both!

Tea, for example, can be prepared in two ways:

Infusion: Place a tablespoon of the herb in a cup and fill it with boiling water. Cover and set aside for ten minutes before serving. In general, medicinal plant leaves and flowers are prepared in this manner.

Cooking: Bring the water to a boil, then add the herb and cook for three minutes. This is how teas made from foraged plants' roots, mushrooms, and other hard parts are made.

Aside from teas, there are many other ways to prepare medicinal herbs, depending on the various traditions that exist around the world, but also on the use you want to give the plant you just foraged:

poultices, compresses, inhalations, ointments, or simply a few leaves in your coffee or tea.

How can medicinal herbs and plants be harvested, dried, and stored in a sustainable manner?

Harvesting, drying, and storing medicinal plants are critical considerations, especially if you are foraging plants that are not available all year. Despite the fact that most plants can be used fresh or dried, but you must know how to dry and store them properly!

Medicinal Plant Harvesting

You must consider the following factors for an abundant and effective collection of aromatic and medicinal plants in the wild:

- The part of the flower that you will use. You might only need to use a plant's flower, fruit, leaves, or root.
- However, you must also consider when the collection is most appropriate, that is when you should do it

Collecting leaves should be done before the flowers fully open.

If you want to collect flowers, do so before they fully open.

If you're going to collect roots, do so before their growing season ends.

If you're going to collect fruits, do so before they reach maturity.

The medicinal plant drying process:

Drying is a critical step in allowing the plant to be used all year. To do this effectively, you must consider the following:

- If you want to dry flowers or leaves, you should do so in the shade.
- When drying roots or thick leaves, place them in the sun to dry.
- If possible, tie them with a rope or hang them on a metal mesh in well-ventilated and dry areas.
- Move them constantly to ensure even drying.
- Protect them from dust and insects.
- Wash the roots thoroughly.

Keep in mind that the plant must retain a minimum percentage of its humidity and must remain green because the yellow color of the leaf indicates that the plant has lost all of its properties.

Basic Knowledge of Medicinal Plants, Herbs, and Flowers

Cattails

Cattail has numerous health benefits, including the ability to act as a toxin filter, reduce bleeding, and provide antiseptic properties.

Mullein

Mullein has numerous health benefits: if you have respiratory issues, you can always make mullein tea. You will feel better in no time.

Nettles

Nettles have numerous health benefits, including the ability to act as a decongestant, to treat prostate diseases, and to act as a diuretic. When trying to detox, some people drink nettle tea.

Rosemary

The leaves are used to make tea. It is used as an infusion for digestive and liver problems, as well as a general tonic for the body. It is also antiseptic and healing when applied externally (as an ointment) (prevents infections from occurring).

Lemon balm

Its leaves are used to make an exquisite digestive infusion as well as a mild sedative.

Oregano

Its leaves are utilized. It is an antispasmodic (relaxes the intestinal muscles, relieving pain) and carminative herb that is very beneficial for digestive disorders (helps to eliminate gas). It acts as an expectorant (helps to eliminate mucus) and is antiseptic and anti-inflammatory in respiratory disorders (Sakkas, 2017).

Thyme

Its leaves are utilized. It is fundamentally antiseptic, making it extremely useful in the treatment of respiratory conditions. It has antispasmodic properties in digestive disorders (Salehi, 2018).

Coriander

The fruits are applied as a poultice to relieve rheumatic pain. You can make infusions or chew it because it promotes gastric juice secretion and aids digestion (Laribi, 2015).

Chamomile

These flowers can be found in the wild. These small and wonderful flowers have numerous benefits, including anti-inflammatory properties for the mouth, throat, eyes, and skin. It is digestive and antispasmodic, as well as sedative and healing. You can make tea to help you feel better (Khalesi, 2019).

Words of Advice

These edible wild plants and the information I've provided are not intended to be substitutes for medical treatment or advice from a licensed physician. If you are about to make significant changes to your lifestyle, please consult your trusted doctor or nutritionist first!

CHAPTER 11

How to Prepare Foraged Food

What a thrill to be almost ready to eat your wild plants! I recall my first taste of dandelion and other types of wild greens salad. I couldn't believe I was getting a healthy lunch for free! I didn't have to pay a dime because I foraged all of my food that day, and I was hooked on foraging for the rest of my life!

However, even if edible wild plants are edible, you must ensure that they are carefully prepared so that you can eat them without difficulty. Sure, some of them don't require cooking, but most of the time you'll need to make a special (and not difficult) preparation to get the most out of the plant's flavor.

So, not only do you need to know what plants are edible before eating them, but you also need to know how to eat them. If you don't, you might have a negative experience that discourages you from becoming a forager.

Whether you are concerned about the quality of food in supermarkets, how much money you spend at the grocery store each week, or if your health is slowly (or rapidly) deteriorating, you should definitely consider eating foraged plants.

Wild edible plants will introduce you to a new world of flavors! Your taste buds will appreciate this new adventure you're embarking on. If you're looking for kitchen inspiration, keep reading!

Begin with Small Bites.

It could be argued that the majority of edible wild plants are safe for most people. However, we are all unique, with unique bio-needs that are determined by our bodies and our lifestyles.

This is why we must remember that plants are different when they are in the wild, whereas we are not (generally).

Speaking of which, I used to eat them all the time.

So, we'll need to first strengthen our immune systems and our bodies responses to the plants we're about to consume because you've never tried those plants before and don't know how they'll affect you.

If this is your first time eating a particular wild plant, only try a small amount of it. You don't want to eat it all in case you're allergic to it or have an unusual reaction to it.

Don't Overexpose Yourself

You've taken the first big step by going out of your way to start foraging for your own food! That in itself is quite impressive. That is why you should limit your exposure and eat large quantities of the new plant you discovered.

I would also advise you to start with one plant per day. So, try dandelions today and see how your body reacts; then, in two days, try wild garlic and see if you have any reactions to it.

This is a precautionary measure because if you become allergic or intolerant to a plant, how will you know which one caused the reaction if you ate four different types of edible wild plants in one day?!

Furthermore, you should consume the same plant for a few days in a row. Sometimes our bodies need more of a substance to understand that they need to get rid of it; thus, your body will not respond negatively on the first day because you ate the plant again, but it will respond negatively on the third day because you ate it again.

You could also try rubbing the plant against your skin, lips, and tongue to see how it feels. If you don't have any issues, you could try eating a small amount of the plant. If, on the other hand, you begin to feel strange or have an immediate reaction, stop consuming it and put it away!

Eat in Moderation

Another possibility is that we begin eating wild plants, believing that they will not harm us because we have not had a negative reaction to them. Then, out of nowhere, we notice a rash on our skin! We realize that the only thing we ate that was different was that edible wild plant.

Things were great when you ate a small amount of the plant. However, when you decided to increase your intake, problems began to emerge. This is due to the fact that some plants can be poisonous if consumed in large quantities. Spinach and Swiss chard, for example, are two of them! They are not found in the wild, but you should be cautious about how much of those plants you consume.

It's finally time to eat.

If everything goes well and your body does not react to your chosen plant, that is fantastic news! You can now begin foraging for that plant whenever you can. Remember to take the following precautions when foraging:

You must thoroughly rinse or wash all of the plants. Make certain that all dirt is removed.

Conduct some research on the plant you foraged. Some edible wild plants will require you to boil them before eating them.

Don't be afraid to eat them right away! We have become so accustomed to adding salt, pepper, or other condiments to our foods that we have forgotten what their true flavor is! So, I recommend that you refrain from using condiments the first few times you eat those plants; this way, you will be able to fully appreciate all of the new flavors.

The only limit is your imagination! You want to go foraging in order to make delicious and nutritious sauces? Take a chance! Or, alternatively,

Do you enjoy preparing traditional dishes with new flavors, herbs, and plants? Do it right now!

What exactly is a healthy person?

Humans should eat in order to feel good. To be healthy, we all require some nutrients. When we do not eat properly, we can see it in our bodies, particularly in our faces.

A healthy person is one who has a positive attitude, enjoys working and having fun, and is eager to try new things. He or she exercises and lives a happy life.

A healthy person is one who, while experiencing pain in the body, takes care of it, looks good, is in good health, and is eager to share with others.

People who are healthy eat well. This does not imply that they eat a lot or a little, but rather that they are aware of the foods that they allow into their bodies.

Recipes for Edible Wild Plants That Are Simple To Make

Wild Garlic Pesto

Pesto, oh pesto! Who doesn't enjoy the aroma? Pesto is one of those sauces that could go on almost anything! Pesto can be added to soups, meats, salads, pasta, and even sandwiches if you're looking for something different.

If you can find some wild nuts, you can use them in your pesto as well. If not, make do with whatever you have:

Ingredients:

- o   20 large wild garlic leaves will suffice for a small container.
- o   30g basil leaves
- o   20 walnuts or any other nuts you come across
- o   Extra virgin olive oil (add as much as you would like).
- o   10g grated parmesan cheese
- o   Salt, pepper, and lemon juice

Simply combine all of the ingredients in your food processor or blender, and you're done! If your pesto is too thick, simply add more oil or a splash of water.

Bread with Wild Garlic and Cheese

Cheese garlic bread is well-known throughout the world! But why not try this recipe with some wild garlic instead? Prepare the bread dough and mince the wild garlic. Combine everything with the cheese and the dough. Place it in the oven for nearly an hour (or until golden brown).

Wild Nuts

All of the wild nuts you collect can be used to make butter. A powerful food processor is required; otherwise, your blender may suffer from the strain of attempting to turn the nuts into butter.

The best part about making your own nut butter is that you can control how much salt or sugar you use (if any), as well as the combination of nuts you use. I've made nut butter with black walnuts and ground peanuts, and it's one of the most delicious combinations I've ever tried! They are also high in protein and healthy fats!

Wild Plums

Bullace, for example. This type of wild plum can be used to make jam or jelly. If you're making jam, use brown sugar to give it that extra special flavor.

Rosemary

It can be used to flavor and season roasts, chickens, and baked lambs, as well as stews and fish.

Lemon balm

It is used in salads as well as to make infusions and juices. It tastes similar to lemon.

Oregano

It is a fragrant condiment for sauces, preserves, pizzas, cooked vegetables, salads, stews, and other dishes. If you are interested in lacto-fermentation techniques, you should include this herb in your preparations; it will improve the taste of everything.

Wild Spinach Meatballs

Ingredients:

- o   untamed spinach
- o   pepper and salt
- o   parsley and oregano
- o   wild onion and garlic
- o   three or four eggs
- o   lemon or vinegar

Cook the wild spinach for a few minutes. When you see that they are cooked, take them out and finely chop them. Season with salt and pepper, oregano, parsley, garlic, wild onion, and eggs. Add the lemon gradually and thoroughly mix everything together. Make the balls into meatballs by rolling them in breadcrumbs or flour.

You can either bake or fry them.

Plantain Omelet

Ingredients:

- o   1 pound plantain
- o   6 eggs
- o   3 tbsp olive oil
- o   4 slices cut potatoes

o   pepper and salt

The potatoes can be steamed or boiled. Separate the eggs and season with salt and pepper. Soak the plantain in vinegar and water, then pat dry. Heat the oil in the pan and add all of the ingredients, including the plantain. When one side is golden brown, flip it over and cook the other side.

Wild vegetables patties Empanadas

Ingredients:

-Any wild vegetables you find and desire.

-Wild onion, parsley, black pepper, and oregano

-Salt and pepper to taste

-Cheese, grated

-2 eggs.

- 1 teaspoon of flour

Bring all of your wild vegetable selections to a boil. Drain well and thinly slice. Slice the onion and season with parsley, pepper, and oregano. Season with salt and pepper to taste.

You can top it with a few tablespoons of grated cheese to make it even more delicious!

Then add an egg or two and a tablespoon of flour to the mixture to bring it all together.

Separately, make the dough for the empanadas with your favorite flour.

Cook the dough with the mixture.

Wild Vegetables Gnocchi

Ingredients:

-Any wild vegetables you have on hand that you want to use.
-Nutmeg, salt, and pepper
-Parsley and garlic
-Cheese, grated
-Flour
-3 eggs

Bring all of your wild vegetables to a boil in a pot. When it's done, let it drain for a few minutes before cutting it. Along with the nutmeg, cheese, three eggs, and flour, you add the salt, pepper, garlic, and chopped parsley to the chopped vegetables.

Form the gnocchi by combining all of the ingredients. Cook in salted water with a little oil.

Chestnut Spread

If you live in an area where chestnuts are plentiful, consider yourself extremely fortunate! You must harvest and cook the nuts before eating them because they are highly toxic if eaten raw, owing to the amount of tannic acid they contain.

Remove the skins from your chestnuts first. They could be boiled or roasted. I prefer roasting them because it is faster. When they are very hot, remove them from the oven and begin peeling them so you can remove the furry skin.

The nut will then appear! Put them all in the food processor and process for a few minutes, or until every single part is crushed, and you'll have your nut butter.

Sour Dandelions Pie

Stuffing ingredients include:

- 1 cup drained dandelions
- 1 thinly sliced wild onion
- 1 teaspoon paprika
- 1 cup ground beef (or soy)
- -Salt, oregano, and parsley
- 1 tablespoon olive oil
- -Grated cheese 2 beaten eggs

Fry the onion with the meat or soybeans. When it is thoroughly cooked, add the dandelion, paprika, parsley, and oregano. Season everything and combine thoroughly. Remove it from the heat when it is done. Mix in a couple of tablespoons of grated cheese and the eggs.

Then, using your favorite flour, make the dough for the sour pie. Place the freshly cooked filling on top and bake for about 30 minutes.

CONCLUSION

If you've decided to read this book, you probably don't care about social norms and are aware of how much nutritional value can be obtained from foraged (and sometimes hidden) plants, herbs, flowers, and nuts.

You're attempting to immerse yourself in the foraging world in order to supplement your diet. You may also want to become healthier and fitter because you care about nature or are looking for a new hobby that is in tune with the surroundings where you are now living.

I just want to thank you for going foraging for whatever reason you did! Thank you for allowing yourself to learn more about this topic, as I am aware it can be taboo among some people. Thank you for conducting research and prioritizing your health. Above all, thank you for taking the time to understand and observe how nature works; we need more people doing this because it also helps mother nature become healthier!

You learned about the characteristics that make a plant edible, non-edible, or poisonous in this book. You also learned where to look for edible wild plants, which areas to avoid, and how to correctly identify plants based on the season.

If you believe you are ready to go foraging, good news! That most likely means you are! Make sure you go foraging in areas where there are no traces of humans, where pesticides or other types of contaminants are not visible (or nonexistent), and where you can go off the beaten path to find abundant edible wild plants that are easily harvested.

Furthermore, going foraging implies that you have grown accustomed to watching the weather forecast for the next few days because you know that after a heavy rain, there are more chances to find and discover new plants that could bring many more great benefits to your lifestyle.

Furthermore, by foraging for edible wild plants, you are helping to preserve places and species of plants, fruits, herbs, nuts, and flowers. You understand that, while nature provides a plentiful supply of food, you cannot (or should not) harvest it all. You become more in tune with the area from which you are harvesting because you are aware of how valuable that produce is because you see its effects firsthand.

Because, without a doubt, once you become a forager and go through a transition period in which your entire lifestyle changes, you will notice how your body, mind, and soul positively react to those changes.

As a result of going foraging, your body changes and becomes healthier; you begin (or continue) to exercise; you ground yourself and spend time in nature; and you become more connected to what you put inside your body.

You become healthier; your mind is clearer, your thoughts are more positive in relation to what you are living and experiencing, and you are resurrecting long-lost knowledge and wisdom.

Your soul changes as you raise awareness about the importance of foraging for edible wild plants and pass through a transitional period. People will notice you are doing something different even if you do not actively go out and invite everyone to come foraging with you. Your energy is being redirected toward a more natural state of being; you are no longer allowing others to dictate what you can and cannot buy and consume; instead, you are taking the lead and making the decisions for yourself!

Certainly, this is a huge responsibility for all of us foragers; however, we are ready and committed to the changes we are attempting and experiencing, because this isn't a "trend" or something we do for the sake of a "photo opportunity." In fact, as foragers, we are looking for a healthier lifestyle that will empower us; a lifestyle that can also contribute to our personal pursuit of health, and where our nutritional needs are met without negatively impacting our environment.

We all had preconceived notions about going foraging. Thoughts like, "What if I get in trouble?" "Or, what if I'm doing it incorrectly?" " were probably running through our heads when we were about to go foraging for the first time. Furthermore, we live in a society where parents frequently warn their children not to touch or eat any wild plants because they are all poisonous. Even if they aren't, they'll say it anyway because they don't know any better.

And this could be a dangerous misconception, especially if we allow it to rule our thoughts and prevent us from foraging. The truth is that when we go foraging for food, we are simply returning to how our ancestors used to live because foraging was a part of their daily lives.

We become self-sufficient when we go foraging because we can find and harvest our own food. And I know that this mindset of returning to nature and finding healthier food options is making a big comeback because we are all opening our eyes to the nutritious plants that are right in front of us.

Foraging for edible wild plants is becoming increasingly popular as time passes. I'm so happy for you and the adventure you're about to embark on! You'll quickly realize that everything you've been eating is nothing compared to what you can find if you go foraging every now and then.

Learning to successfully forage can and will completely transform your life. You will learn new skills, broaden your knowledge, pay closer attention, and understand how

Nature is amazing, and you will be able to gather not only food but also medicine for free!

And, may I just point out the best part about foraging for edible wild plants? Those plants are chock-full of nutrients, antioxidants, minerals, and even water! If you eat edible wild plants, you can meet all of your basic needs. Can you imagine how much better your health would be if you went foraging while also maintaining your lifestyle?

I'll never forget the first time I decided to go foraging. Even though I wasn't wearing the most comfortable clothes, I decided it was time to get my hands dirty in the dirt. I used to believe that "foraging is pointless because you can't really find anything to eat unless you buy it from a farmer's market or a supermarket." Oh, how naive I was. I knew very little about nature and the natural processes that occur, and how we can take advantage of them.

After that first experience, I became obsessed with going foraging because I wanted to learn everything I could to satisfy my soul. And hopefully, you'll be inspired to go foraging as well!

As you can see, going foraging for edible wild plants is not only a fun activity to do with others, but it will also bring you closer to nature and those around you, teach you how nature works, and give you a clear picture of how little we really need to live a successful and healthy lifestyle.

Going foraging does not imply that you will simply gather some food and leave. It implies that you care about the environment and want to reduce your carbon footprint (and you manage to do this by buying less at the supermarket and by finding your food out in nature).

But you also do this once you begin to appreciate what you can find outside even more because you are feeding yourself and those you care about in a very sustainable way that is in sync with nature and its cycles. In fact, every time you forage, you will be helping nature and harvest an invasive species in that ecosystem to ensure that other native plants can thrive in that area without having to struggle or fight against the foreign plants.

I truly hope you go foraging for edible wild plants; you will not be disappointed! May your baskets always be filled with foraged edible wild plants!

www.ingramcontent.com/pod-product-compliance
Lightning Source LLC
LaVergne TN
LVHW020815200726
843506LV00009B/1056

9 783986 537456